FRENCH GCSE

REVISION QUICKIES

ENVIRONMENT, HEALTH & CAREER

ACKNOWLEDGEMENTS

Our heartfelt thanks to our team of guest proofreaders: Aurélie Lethuilier, Nadim Cham and Jérôme Nogues. Their contributions have ensured not only a highly accurate book, but also helped make some improvements in terms of choice of lexis. Thank you for lending your time and expertise to this project.

Our gratitude to Martin Lapworth for his time spent creating online versions of the Sentence Builders books linked to the Revision Quickies series. These are now available, via subscription, on SentenceBuilders.com. Thank you.

Lastly, thanks to all the wonderful, supportive and passionate educators on Twitter who have helped enhance our books with their suggestions and comments, and to the members of the Global Innovative Language Teachers (GILT) Facebook group for their engagement with the Sentence Builders series. We consider ourselves very lucky to have such colleagues to inspire and spur us on.

ISBN:

Imprint: Independently Published
Edited by Dylan Viñales

THE LANGUAGE GYM

ABOUT THIS BOOK

As the title clearly suggests, this resource is intended for GCSE exam revision with a focus on the consolidation of high-frequency and high-surrender-value words and lexical chunks. Since the content closely matches the vocabulary included in our French GCSE Revision, " Environment, Health & Career" the two books should be used together for best results.

The design of the 'quickies' is based on the key principle that durable vocabulary learning is more likely to occur when lexical items are processed deeply, repeatedly and at every level of grain, i.e. meaning, syntax, lexicogrammar, orthography. Accordingly, each quickie recycles the key vocabulary several times over; builds word associations; elicits deeper level of cognitive investment on the part of the learners and includes tasks which involve semantic processing and others which involve a focus on collocations, colligations, grammar and spelling. In order to cater for differentiated learning, we have included two sets of quickies per unit: a foundation-level set and a higher-level set, the latter including more challenging vocabulary and tasks.

Each unit ends with a productive retrieval-practice assessment which may be used to test summatively the uptake of the vocabulary practiced in each unit or merely as an extra revision tool.

The revision quickie's format has been tried and tested for years, and is based on the huge success of Dr Gianfranco Conti's GCSE French and Spanish revision quickies, the most downloaded language learning resources of all times on www.tes.com.

We hope both you and your students find this book useful.

Gianfranco, Ronan & Dylan

TABLE OF CONTENTS

Unit 1. Food and eating out

KEY VOCABULARY Foundation

1. La nourriture *(food)*

La confiture: *Jam*
La glace: *Ice cream*
La salade: *Salad*
La viande: *Meat*
Le fromage: *Cheese*
Le gâteau: *Cake*
Le jambon: *Ham*
Le pain: *Bread*
Le poisson: *Fish*
Le poulet: *Chicken*
Le riz: *Rice*
Le sucre: *Sugar*
Les champignons: *Mushrooms*
Les épinards: *Spinach*
Les fraises: *Strawberries*
Les fritures: *Fried foods*
Les fruits de mer: *Seafood*
Les frites: *Fries*
Les légumes: *Vegetables*
Les œufs: *Eggs*
Les pâtes: *Pasta*
Les pommes: *Apples*
Les pommes de terre: *Potatoes*
Les sucreries: *Sweets*
Les viennoiseries: *Pastries*

2. Les boissons *(drinks)*

La bière: *Beer*
L'eau (minérale): *(Mineral) water*
Le jus de fruits: *Fruit juice*
Le vin blanc: *White wine*
Le vin rouge: *Red wine*
Les boissons gazeuses: *Fizzy drinks*

3. Les verbes importants

Aimer: *To like*
Boire: *To drink*
Commander: *To order*
Manger: *To eat*
Prendre: *To have*
Vouloir: *To want*

4. Les expressions essentielles

J'adore: *I love*
J'ai envie de: *I want*
J'aime (beaucoup): *I like (a lot)*
Je n'aime pas: *I don't like*
Je ne supporte pas: *I can't stand*
Je voudrais: *I would like*

1. Gapped translation

a. J'aime le bœuf: *I like* ________
b. Je ne veux pas de frites: *I* ______ ________ *any fries*
c. J'adore le poisson: *I love* ___________
d. Je ne mange pas de fruits de mer: *I don't eat* __________
e. J'aime beaucoup les fraises: *I like* _______________ *a lot*
f. Je n'aime pas le sucre: *I don't like* ________
g. Je mange de la salade: *I eat* _________
h. J'adore les pommes de terre: *I love* ____________
i. Je ne mange pas de viennoiseries: *I don't eat* _________

2. Complete the table

English	Français
Pastries	
	J'aime les fruits de mer
Ice cream	
	J'adore les légumes
	Je déteste les œufs
Sweets	
	Je ne mange pas de bœuf
Fried foods	

3. Categories: sort the words below in the appropriate category

a. Gâteaux – b. Épinards – c. Pommes – d. Pommes de terre
e. Vin rouge – f. Champignons – g. Fraises – h. Bonbons
i. Eau – j. Jus – k. Viennoiseries

Fruits	Légumes	Sucreries	Boissons

4. Faulty translation: be careful, some are correct!

a. Je ne suppporte pas: *I don't like*

b. Je ne mange pas de sucreries: *I don't eat fried foods*

c. Je ne bois pas de vin blanc: *I don't drink red wine*

d. J'adore les pommes de terre: *I love apples*

e. Je bois beaucoup d'eau: *I drink a lot of water*

f. Je ne mange jamais de viennoiseries: *I never eat pasta*

g. Je voudrais du sucre: *I would like some salt*

h. J'ai envie de fraises: *I want some strawberries*

5. Match

Viennoiseries	***Apple juice***
Légumes	***Pasta***
Boire	***Water***
Pommes de terre	***To like***
Gâteaux	***Meat***
Poisson	***Wine***
Viande	***Fish***
Aimer	***Cakes***
Pâtes	***Potatoes***
Vin	***Vegetables***
Eau	***Pastries***
Jus de pomme	***To drink***

6. Broken words

a. J'aime la vian_ _ : *I like meat*

b. Je ne mange pas de lég_ _ _ _ :
I don't eat vegetables

c. Je ne supporte pas les épin_ _ _ _ :
I can't stand spinach

d. Je voudrais du j_ _ de pomme:
I would like some apple juice

e. J'ai envie de la bi_ _ _ :
I want beer

f. Je prends du vin rou_ _ :
I have red wine

g. Je ne mange pas de sucr_ _ _ _ _ :
I don't eat sweets

h. Je prends des fritu_ _ _ :
I have fried foods

7. Translate into English

a. Je ne prends pas de légumes
b. Je ne supporte pas les épinards
c. J'adore le poisson
d. J'aime beaucoup les pâtes
e. Je ne mange pas de poisson
f. Je mange souvent des fruits de mer
g. Je ne bois pas de vin ou de bière
h. Au déjeuner, je prends une salade
i. Au dîner, je mange du poulet
j. Au petit-déjeuner, je prends un œuf

8. Sentence puzzle

a. parents Mes mangent de viande beaucoup:
My parents eat a lot of meat

b. de Je l'eau voudrais: *I would like some water*

c. petit-déjeuner je des oeufs Au prends
For breakfast, I have eggs

d. voudrais Je de minérale l'eau
I would like some mineral water

e. légumes Je ne pas mange de: *I don't eat vegetables*

f. de Je bois pas bière ne: *I don't drink beer*

g. voudrais Je pomme jus du de:
I would like some apple juice

9. Complete with de/du/de la/de l' or des as appropriate

a. J'ai envie de manger _____ viande

b. Je voudrais _____ eau

c. Au déjeuner, je prends _____ pâtes et _____ poisson

d. Je ne mange pas _____ légumes

e. Mes parents mangent beaucoup _____ sucreries

f. Vous voulez _____ vin?

g. Je ne bois pas _____ bière

h. Je voudrais _____ jus de pomme

10. Word-level translation into French

a. *Eggs*: .	g. *To like*:
b. *Spinach*:	h. *To drink*:
c. *Vegetables*:	i. *To eat*:
d. *Sweets*:	j. *I would like*:
e. *Water*:	k. *I don't eat*:
f. *Fried foods*:	l. *I want*:

11. Sentence-level translation into French

a. I can't stand spinach, I prefer mushrooms
b. I like pasta a lot. I also like bread and rice
c. I would like some apple juice
d. I can't stand vegetables, but I eat fruit
e. I want sweets this evening
f. For dinner, I usually have fish and potatoes
g. For breakfast, I usually have eggs and ham
h. For lunch, I usually have meat and vegetables or fries
i. I don't like meat, but I love fish and seafood
j. I would like to order a fruit juice

KEY VOCABULARY Higher

1. Les repas *(meals)*

Pour le petit-déjeuner: *For breakfast*

Pour le déjeuner, je mange: *For lunch, I eat*

Pour le goûter, je bois: *For snack, I drink*

Pour le dîner, je prends: *For dinner, I have*

La nourriture *(food)* et les boissons *(drinks)*

Le bœuf: *Beef*

Le canard: *Duck*

L'eau: *Water*

Les boissons gazeuses: *Fizzy drinks*

Les crevettes: *Prawns*

Les fritures: *Fried foods*

Les fruits de mer: *Seafood*

2. Les adjectifs pour décrire la nourriture

Bon: *Good*

Épicé: *Spicy*

Exquis: *Outstanding*

Fade: *Bland*

Gras: *Greasy*

Nourrissant: *Nutritious*

Sain: *Healthy*

Salé: *Salty*

Savoureux: *Tasty*

Succulent: *Succulent*

Sucré: *Sweet*

3. Pour intensifier *(to intensify)*

Assez: *Quite*

Plutôt: *Rather*

Très: *Very*

Trop: *Too*

Vraiment: *Really*

4. Dire *(say)* ce que je veux commander

J'aimerais commander: *I would like to order*

Je voudrais boire: *I would like to drink*

Nous voudrions manger: *We would like to eat*

5. Dire ce que j'aime/je n'aime pas

Ce dont j'ai horreur: *What I have a horror of*

Ce que j'aime le moins: *What I like the least*

Ce que j'aime le plus: *What I like the most*

Ce que j'aime manger: *What I like eating*

Ce que je déteste manger: *What I hate eating*

Ce que je ne supporte pas: *What I can't stand*

Ma nourriture préférée: *My favourite food*

Mon plat préféré, c'est: *My favourite dish is*

1. Match up

Les repas	***Seafood***
Les fruits de mer	***Snack***
Le déjeuner	***To drink***
Commander	***Good***
La nourriture	***Greasy***
Épicé	***Food***
Les crevettes	***Prawns***
Bon	***Lunch***
Sucré	***Sweet***
Gras	***Meals***
Boire	***To order***
Le goûter	***Spicy***

2. Gapped translation

a. Nous aimerions _______________ de l'eau:
We would like to order some water

b. Je voudrais _____________ un hamburger:
I would like to buy a burger

c. Pour le _________, je prends __ _________ chaud:
For breakfast, I have some hot chocolate

d. Ce que j'aime ___ ______, c'est le ___________ :
What I like the least is cheese

e. Ce dont j'ai __________, ce sont les __________ :
What I have a horror of are vegetables

f. Ce que j'aime le _____ , ce ______ les _________ :
What I like the most are prawns

g. Je voudrais _____________ du bœuf bourguignon:
I would like to eat some beef bourguignon

h. Ce que je ne ________ pas, ce ____ les ________ :
What I can't stand is fried foods

3. Missing consonants

a. _ _o_ : *too*

b. _o_ _a_ _e_ : *to order*

c. _ _u_ô_ : *rather*

d._ a_ou_eu_ : *tasty*

e. _oi_e: *to drink*

f. _ai_ : healthy

g. _ _ai_e_ _ : *really*

h. _ou_ _i_u_e: *food*

i. _ _e_e_ _e_ : *prawns*

j. _u_ _é: *sweet*

4. Broken words

a. creve_____ : *prawns*

b. épi_____ : *spicy*

c. tr___ : *too (much)*

d. su_____ : *sweet*

e. vrai_____ : *really*

f. boi___ : *to drink*

g. savou______ : *tasty*

h. nour_______ : *food*

i. man______ : *to eat*

j. sa___ : *healthy*

5. Spot and fix the incorrect translations. PLEASE NOTE: not all the sentences contain mistakes!

a. Ma nourriture préférée: *My favourite drink*

b. Ce que je ne supporte pas: *What I can't stand*

c. J'adore la nourriture épicée: *I love spicy food*

d. Pour le goûter, je prends: *For dinner, I have*

e. C'est assez sain: *It's quite healthy*

f. C'est trop salé: *It's too bland*

g. Nous aimerions commander: *We would like to order*

h. Je voudrais acheter: *You would like to buy*

i. Ce que j'aime le moins: *What I like the most*

j. Mon plat préféré: *My favourite snack*

k. C'est vraiment bon: *It's really bad*

l. Le bœuf est exquis: *The beef is outstanding*

6. Anagrams

a. turerriNou:

b. ûterGo:

c. quisEx:

d. entaimVr:

e. mdermanCo:

f. cépiÉ:

g. atPl:

h. euxvouSar:

7. Sentence puzzle

a. la nourriture J'adore épicée:

b. que le viande plus, c'est j'aime la Ce:

c. bon vraiment C'est:

d. voudrais Je café commander un:

e. de les J'adore mer fruits:

f. trop Le est salé boeuf:

g. prends le goûter, je un Pour sandwich:

h. supporte Ce je légumes ne pas, ce que les sont:

8. Complete the table

English	Français
What I like the least	
	La nourriture épicée
	La nourriture sucrée
We would like	
	Commander de l'eau
I have seafood	
	Ce que j'aime le plus
It's too salty	
It's very healthy	

9. Find in the wordsearch the French for the words listed in the box below

T	B	O	N	H	R	V
R	F	A	D	E	K	R
O	A	T	C	S	E	A
P	G	Z	V	A	X	I
A	R	P	W	I	Q	M
S	A	L	É	N	U	E
L	S	A	P	Q	I	N
M	Y	T	I	I	S	T
E	R	H	C	B	P	V
F	B	U	É	P	O	E
L	C	B	O	I	R	E

Good: B
Healthy: S
Really: V
Spicy: É
Too: T
Oustanding: E
To drink: B
Bland: F
Dish: P
Greasy: G

10. Guided translation

a. *Some drinks*: D___ b__________

b. *Too salty*: T____ s_________

c. *For lunch*: P____ l__ d____________

d. *Really good*: V__________ b____

e. *Very healthy*: T____ s_______

f. *We would like*: N____ v___________

g. *For snack*: P___ l__ g___________

h. *I can't stand*: J_ n_ s___________ p___

i. *It's bland*: C'____ f______

j. *Spicy food*: D_ l_ n__________ é_______

k. *I would like*: J___ v__________

11. Translate into French

a. For breakfast, I have some eggs and some fruit

b. For lunch, I have fish and some vegetables

c. For snack, I have a cheese sandwich and a coffee

d. What I can't stand are fizzy drinks and fries

e. I don't like burgers because it's too greasy

f. What I love is fried foods, but it's not healthy

g. What I like the most is beef because it's tasty

h. What I like the least are prawns and vegetables

i. I would like to eat seafood and drink water

j. I love spicy and salty food. I don't like sweet food

UNIT 1 - Test (/100)

1. Vocabulary recognition: French-to-English gapped translation (/15)

a. Mon plat préféré, c'est le bœuf bourguignon: *My favourite* ________ *is* ________ *bourguignon*

b. Ce que j'aime le plus, c'est le poulet: ________ *I like* ________, *is* ___________

c. Pour le déjeuner, je ne mange pas de viande: *For* _________ *I don't* ________ *any* __________

d. J'adore les fruits de mer, mais je n'aime pas le poisson: *I love* ___________, *but I don't like* _______

e. J'aimerais commander de l'eau et du fromage: *I* ____________ *to* _____ *water and some*__________

f. Nous voudrions manger des légumes ce soir: *We would like to eat some* __________ *this* ________

2. Syntax/Lexicogrammar – Split sentences (/5)

Ce que j'aime le plus, ce	prenons une salade ou un morceau de fromage
Pour le petit-déjeuner, d'habitude je	poulet rôti avec des pommes de terre
Mon plat préféré, ce sont les	sont les fruits de mer
Le soir, on ne mange pas beaucoup. Nous	mange du pain grillé avec du miel
J'aimerais commander du	légumes farcis à la provençale

3. Grammar/Morphology/Vocabulary – Tangled translation (/20)

a. Je voudrais **some bread**

b. Ce **of which** j'ai horreur, ce sont les **prawns**

c. Ma **food favourite**, c'est le poisson

d. Ces **pasta** sont vraiment **good**

e. Pour le déjeuner, nous **take** des **eggs**

f. Hier, j'ai **drunk some water**

g. Pour le petit-déjeuner, nous **drink some** thé

h. Ce **which** j'aime le plus, ce sont **the** pâtes

i. **This** matin, **I ate** du riz

j. Pour le dîner, nous **eat some** légumes

4. Translate into French (/ 60 – each full sentence – 6 points)

a. What I like the most is cheese

b. For dinner, we eat meat or fish

c. What I have a horror of are vegetables

d. I would like to buy some meat for my lunch

e. I love cheese because it's very tasty

f. Honey is quite sweet and healthy

g. What I can't stand is greasy food

h. The chicken is outstanding, but the rice is bland

i. I eat eggs because they are nutritious

j. I don't eat sugar because it isn't healthy

Unit 1. Food and eating out - Foundation - Answers

1. Gapped translation

a. *I like **beef*** b. *I **don't want** any fries* c. *I love **fish*** d. *I don't eat **seafood*** e. *I like **strawberries** a lot*
f. *I don't like **sugar*** g. *I eat **salad*** h. *I love **potatoes*** i. *I don't eat **pastries***

2. Complete the table

Pastries **-** Viennoiseries ***I like seafood*** **-** J'aime les fruits de mer ***Ice cream*** **-** La glace
I love vegetables **-** J'adore les légumes ***I hate eggs*** **-** Je déteste les œufs ***Sweets*** **-** Les sucreries
I don't eat beef **-** Je ne mange pas de bœuf *Fried foods* - **Les fritures**

3. Categories: sort the words below in the appropriate category

Fruits: **Pommes / Fraises** Légumes: **Épinards / Pommes de terre / Champignons**
Sucreries: **Gâteaux / Bonbons / Viennoiseries** Boissons: **Vin rouge / Eau / Jus**

4. Faulty translation: be careful, some are correct!

a. Je ne suppporte pas: *I **can't stand*** b. Je ne mange pas de sucreries: *I don't eat **sweets***
c. Je ne bois pas de vin blanc: *I don't drink **white** wine* d. J'adore les pommes de terre: *I love **potatoes***
e. Je bois beaucoup d'eau: *I drink a lot of water* √ f. Je ne mange jamais de viennoiseries: *I never eat **pastries***
g. Je voudrais du sucre: *I would like some **sugar*** h. J'ai envie de fraises: *I want some strawberries* √

5. Match

Viennoiseries – ***Pastries*** Légumes – ***Vegetables*** Boire – ***To drink*** Pommes de terre – ***Potatoes***
Gâteaux – ***Cakes*** Poisson – ***Fish*** Viande – ***Meat*** Aimer – ***To like*** Pâtes – ***Pasta***
Vin – ***Wine*** Eau – ***Water*** Jus de pomme – ***Apple juice***

6. Broken words

a. J'aime la vian**de** b. Je ne mange pas de lég**umes** c. Je ne supporte pas les épin**ards**
d. Je voudrais du j**us** de pomme e. J'ai envie de la bi**ère** f. Je prends du vin rou**ge**
g. Je ne mange pas de sucr**eries** h. Je prends des fritu**res**

7. Translate into English

a. I don't have vegetables b. I can't stand spinach c. I love fish d. I like pasta a lot e. I don't eat fish
f. I often eat seafood g. I don't drink any wine or any beer h. For lunch, I have a salad
i. At dinner, I eat chicken j. At breakfast, I have an egg

8. Sentence puzzle

a. Mes parents mangent beaucoup de viande b. Je voudrais de l'eau
c. Au petit-déjeuner, je prends des d. Je voudrais de l'eau minérale
e. Je ne mange pas de légumes f. Je ne bois pas de bière
g. Je voudrais du jus de pomme

9. Complete with de/du/de l' or des as appropriate

a. **de la** b. **de l'** c. **des** / **du** d. **de** e. **de** f. **du** g. **de** h. **du**

10. Word-level translation into French

a. **Œufs** b. **Épinards** c. **Légumes** d. **Sucreries** e. **Eau** f. **Fritures** g. **Aimer**
h. **Boire** i. **Manger** j. **Je voudrais** k. **Je ne mange pas** l. **Je veux**

11. Sentence-level translation into French

a. Je ne supporte pas les épinards, je préfère les champignons
b. J'aime beaucoup les pâtes. J'aime aussi le pain et le riz
c. Je voudrais du jus de pomme
d. Je ne supporte pas les légumes, mais je mange des fruits
e. Je veux des sucreries ce soir
f. Pour le dîner, d'habitude je prends du poisson et des pommes de terre
g. Pour le petit-déjeuner, d'habitude je prends des œufs et du jambon
h. Pour le déjeuner, d'habitude je prends de la viande et des légumes ou des frites
i. Je n'aime pas la viande, mais j'adore le poisson et les fruits de mer
j. Je voudrais commander un jus de fruits

Unit 1. Food and eating out - Higher - Answers

1. Match up
Les repas – **Meals** Les fruits de mer – **Seafood** Le déjeuner – **Lunch** Commander – **To order**
La nourriture – **Food** Épicé – **Spicy** Les crevettes – **Prawns** Bon – **Good** Sucré – **Sweet**
Gras – **Greasy** Boire – **To drink** Le goûter – **Snack**

2. Gapped translation
a. Nous aimerions **commander** de l'eau b. Je voudrais **acheter** un hamburger
c. Pour le **petit-déjeuner**, je prends **du chocolat** chaud d. Ce que j'aime **le moins**, c'est le **fromage**
e. Ce dont j'ai **horreur** ce sont les **légumes** f. Ce que j'aime le **plus**, ce **sont** les **crevettes**
g. Je voudrais **manger** du bœuf bourguignon h. Ce que je ne **supporte** pas, ce **sont** les **fritures**

3. Missing consonants
a. **trop**: *too* b. **commander**: *to order* c. **plutôt**: *rather* d. **savoureux**: *tasty* e. **boire**: *to drink*
f. **sain**: healthy g. **vraiment**: *really* h. **nourriture**: *food* i. **crevettes**: *prawns* j. **sucré**: *sweet*

4. Broken words
a. crevet**tes**: *prawns* b. épi**cé**: *spicy* c. tr**op**: *too (much)* d. su**cré**: *sweet* e. vrai**ment**: *really*
f. boi**re**: *to drink* g. savour**eux**: *tasty* h. nour**riture**: *food* i. man**ger**: *to eat* j. s**ain**: *healthy*

5. Spot and fix the incorrect translations. PLEASE NOTE: not all the sentences contain mistakes!
a. Ma nourriture préférée: *My favourite* ***food***
b. Ce que je ne supporte pas: *What I can't stand*
c. J'adore la nourriture épicée: *I love spicy food*
d. Pour le goûter, je prends: *For* ***snack****, I have*
e. C'est assez sain: *It's quite healthy*
f. C'est trop salé: *It's too* ***salty***
g. Nous aimerions commander: *We would like to order*
h. Je voudrais acheter: ***I*** *would like to buy*
i. Ce que j'aime le moins: *What I like the* ***least***
j. Mon plat préféré: *My favourite* ***dish***
k. C'est vraiment bon: *It's really* ***good***
l. Le bœuf est exquis: *The beef is outstanding*

6. Anagrams
a. Nourriture b. Goûter c. Exquis d. Vraiment e. Commander f. Épicé g. Plat h. Savoureux

7. Sentence puzzle
a. J'adore la nourriture épicée b. Ce que j'aime le plus, c'est la viande c. C'est vraiment bon
d. Je voudrais commander un café e. J'adore les fruits de mer f. Le boeuf est trop salé
g. Pour le goûter, je prends un sandwich h. Ce que je ne supporte pas, ce sont les légumes

8. Complete the table
What I like the least: **Ce que j'aime le moins** ***Spicy food***: La nourriture épicée
Sweet food: La nourriture sucrée *We would like*: **Nous aimerions/voudrions**
To order water: Commander de l'eau *I have seafood*: **Je prends des fruits de mer**
What I like the most: Ce que j'aime le plus *It's too salty*: **C'est trop salé** *It's very healthy*: **C'est très sain**

9. Find in the wordsearch the French for the words listed in the box below
Good: **Bon** *Healthy*: **Sain** *Really*: **Vraiment** *Spicy*: **Épicé** *Too*: **Trop** *Oustanding*: **Exquis**
To drink: **Boire** *Bland*: **Fade** *Dish*: **Plat** *Greasy*: **Gras**

10. Guided translation
a. *Some drinks*: **Des boissons** b. *Too salty*: **Trop salé** c. *For lunch*: **Pour le déjeuner**
d. *Really good*: **Vraiment bon** e. *Very healthy*: **Très sain** f. *We would like*: **Nous voudrions**
g. *For snack*: **Pour le goûter** h. *I can't stand*: **Je ne supporte pas** i. *It's bland*: **C'est fade**
j. *Spicy food*: **De la nourriture épicée** k. *I would like*: **Je voudrais**

11. Translate into French
a. Pour le petit-déjeuner, je prends des œufs et des fruits
b. Pour le déjeuner, je prends du poisson et des légumes
c. Pour le goûter, je prends un sandwich au fromage et un café
d. Ce que je ne supporte pas, ce sont les boissons gazeuses et les frites
e. Je n'aime pas les hamburgers parce que c'est trop gras
f. Ce que j'adore ce sont les fritures, mais ce n'est pas sain
g. Ce que j'aime le plus, c'est le bœuf parce que c'est savoureux
h. Ce que j'aime le moins, ce sont les crevettes et les légumes
i. Je voudrais manger des fruits de mer et boire de l'eau
j. J' adore la nourriture épicée et salée. Je n'aime pas la nourriture sucrée

UNIT 1 - Test - Answers (/100)

1. Vocabulary recognition: French-to-English gapped translation (/15)

a. Mon plat préféré, c'est le bœuf bourguignon: *My favourite* ***dish*** *is* ***beef*** *bourguignon*

b. Ce que j'aime le plus, c'est le poulet: ***What*** *I like* ***the most****, is* ***chicken***

c. Pour le déjeuner, je ne mange pas de viande: *For* ***lunch****, I don't* ***eat*** *any* ***meat***

d. J'adore les fruits de mer, mais je n'aime pas le poisson: *I love* ***seafood****, but I don't like* ***fish***

e. J'aimerais commander de l'eau et du fromage: *I* ***would like*** *to* ***order*** *water and some* ***cheese***

f. Nous voudrions manger des légumes ce soir: *We would like to eat some* ***vegetables*** *this* ***evening***

2. Syntax/Lexicogrammar – Split sentences (/5)

Ce que j'aime le plus, ce	**sont les fruits de mer**
Pour le petit-déjeuner, d'habitude je	**mange du pain grillé avec du miel**
Mon plat préféré, ce sont les	**légumes farcis à la provençale**
Le soir, on ne mange pas beaucoup. Nous	**prenons une salade ou un morceau de fromage**
J'aimerais commander du	**poulet rôti avec des pommes de terre**

3. Grammar/Morphology/Vocabulary – Tangled translation (/20)

a. Je voudrais **du** **pain**

b. Ce **dont** j'ai horreur, ce sont les **crevettes**

c. Ma **nourriture** **préférée**, c'est le poisson

d. Ces **pâtes** sont vraiment **bonnes**

e. Pour le déjeuner, nous **prenons** des **œufs**

f. Hier, j'ai **bu** **de l'eau**

g. Pour le petit-déjeuner, nous **buvons** **du** thé

h. Ce **que** j'aime le plus, ce sont **les** pâtes

i. **Ce** matin, **j'ai mangé** du riz

j. Pour le dîner, nous **mangeons** **des** légumes

4. Translate into French (/ 60 – each full sentence – 6 points)

a. **Ce que j'aime le plus, c'est le fromage**

b. **Pour le dîner, nous mangeons de la viande ou du poisson**

c. **Ce dont j'ai horreur, ce sont les légumes**

d. **Je voudrais acheter de la viande pour mon déjeuner**

e. **J'adore le fromage parce que c'est très savoureux**

f. **Le miel est assez sucré et sain**

g. **Ce que je ne supporte pas c'est la nourriture grasse**

h. **Le poulet est exquis, mais le riz est fade**

i. **Je mange des œufs parce qu' ils sont nourrissants**

j. **Je ne mange pas de (2) sucre parce que ce n'est pas sain**

Unit 2. Healthy/unhealthy living

KEY VOCABULARY Foundation

1. Les bonnes habitudes *(good habits)*
Je dors huit heures par nuit
I sleep eight hours per night
J'évite les fritures: *I avoid fried foods*
Je fais de l'exercice régulièrement
I exercise regularly
Je mange cinq portions de fruits et légumes par jour
I eat five portions of fruit and vegetables per day
Je me détends: *I relax*
Je ne mange pas trop de matières grasses
I don't eat too much fat
Je ne passe pas trop de temps sur mon ordinateur/portable
I don't spend too much time on my computer/mobile
Je ne prends pas de drogues
I don't take any drugs
Je sors avec mes amis
I go out with my friends
Je suis un régime alimentaire sain
I follow a healthy diet

2. Les mauvaises habitudes *(bad habits)*
Je bois beaucoup d'alcool
I drink a lot of alcohol
Je bois beaucoup de boissons gazeuses
I drink a lot of fizzy drinks
Je fume: I smoke
Je mange beaucoup de sucreries
I eat a lot of sweets
Je ne dors pas assez: *I don't sleep enough*
Je ne fais pas de sport: *I don't do sport*
Je passe des heures sur ma PlayStation
I spend hours on my PlayStation
Je passe trop de temps sur les réseaux sociaux
I spend too much time on social media
Je prends des drogues: *I take drugs*
Je suis toujours stressé(e) *I'm always stressed*

3. Les adjectifs utiles *(useful)*
Bon: *Good*
Dangereux: *Dangerous*
Équilibré: *Balanced*
Fatigué: *Tired*
Gras: *Greasy*
Malsain: *Unhealthy*
Mauvais: *Bad*
Nocif: *Harmful*
Sain: *Healthy*
Sucré: *Sweet*

1. Match up (section 1)

Je dors	***I avoid***
J'évite	***I go out***
Je ne mange pas	***Fried foods***
Les fritures	***I sleep***
Je me détends	***A diet***
Les matières grasses	***I relax***
Sur mon ordinateur	***I don't eat***
Je sors	***On my computer***
Je fais de l'exercice	***Fat***
Un régime alimentaire	***I exercise***

2. Gapped translation (section 1)

a. J'évite les fritures: *I avoid* _______________

b. Je ne mange pas trop de matières grasses:
I don't eat too much _______

c. Je suis un régime alimentaire sain:
I follow a __________ *diet*

d. Je mange cinq portions de fruits et légumes par jour:
I eat five portions of fruit and _____________ *per day*

e. Je fais de l'exercice: *I* ____________

f. Je me détends après l'école: *I* __________ *after school*

g. Je ne prends pas de drogues: *I don't take* _________

3. Complete the sentences with a suitable verb, then translate them into English (section 2)

a. Je ________ beaucoup d'alcool

b. Je ________ toujours stressé

c. Je ________ des sucreries

d. Je ________ beaucoup de cigarettes

e. Je _______ beaucoup de temps sur les réseaux sociaux

f. Je ______ beaucoup de Coca et de Fanta

4. Tick every sentence which refers to a healthy habit

a. Je bois beaucoup d'alcool
b. Je passe huit heures par jour sur mon ordinateur
c. Je passe des heures sur les réseaux sociaux
d. Je mange beaucoup de fritures et de sucreries
e. Je prends cinq portions de légumes par jour
f. J'évite les fritures

5. Complete the table (section 1)

English	Français
I sleep eight hours per night	
	Je me détends
	Je ne mange pas trop de matières grasses
I follow a healthy diet	
	Je sors avec mes amis
I don't take any drugs	
I exercise regularly	
	J'évite les fritures

6. Broken words (section 3)

a. Sa_ _ : *Healthy*

b. Mal_ _ _ _ : *Unhealthy*

c. B_ _ : *Good*

d. No_ _ _ : *Harmful*

e. Dan_ _ _ _ _ _ _ : *Dangerous*

f. _ _ _ré: *Sweet*

g. Mau_ _ _ _ : *Bad*

h. É_ _ _libré: *Balanced*

i. _ _ _ _gué: *Tired*

j. Gr_ _ : *Greasy*

7. Gapped English-to-French translation

a. *I sleep eight hours per night*: Je _______ huit heures par _______

b. *I don't smoke cigarettes*: Je ne _______ pas ___ cigarettes

c. *I avoid fried foods*: J'évite les ___________

d. *I spend hours on social media*:
Je _______ des ________ sur les _________ ________

e. *I exercise regularly*: Je ______ de l'exercice _______________

f. *Fried foods are unhealthy*: Les fritures sont ____________

g. *I eat five portions of vegetables*: Je mange cinq portions de ______

h. *I go out with my friends*: Je ______ avec mes _________

i. *I drink a lot of alcohol*: Je ________ beaucoup d'__________

j. *I don't sleep enough*: Je ne ________ pas _________

8. Spot and supply the one word missing in each sentence

a. Je huit heures par nuit

b. Je ne pas de cigarettes

c. Les fritures mauvaises pour la santé

d. Je passe beaucoup de temps sur les sociaux

e. Je un régime alimentaire très sain

f. Je ne mange pas sucreries

9. Guided translation

a. *Good*: B_ _

b. *Bad*: M_ _ _ _ _ _

c. *Healthy*: S_ _ _

d. *Greasy*: G_ _ _

e. *Harmful*: N_ _ _ _

f. *Sweet*: S_ _ _ _

g. *Tired*: F_ _ _ _ _ _

h. *Drugs*: D_ _ _ _ _ _

i. *Time*: T_ _ _ _

j. *Health*: S_ _ _ _

10. Translate into French

a. I sleep at least eight hours per night

b. I am always tired and stressed

c. I don't smoke cigarettes

d. I avoid fried foods and sweets

e. I spend a lot of time on social media and on my mobile phone

f. I follow a healthy diet

g. I exercise regularly, but I eat a lot of sweets

h. I don't take any drugs, but I smoke sometimes

i. I eat five portions of fruit and vegetables per day

j. I don't drink fizzy drinks

k. Fries are unhealthy and greasy

l. I spend one hour a day on the internet

KEY VOCABULARY Higher

1. Ce que je fais pour rester en forme *(what I do to stay in shape)*

Il faut... *It is necessary to...*

J'essaye de... *I try to...*

-boire beaucoup d'eau: *drink a lot of water*

-dormir huit heures par nuit: *sleep 8 hours a night*

-éviter de fumer: *avoid smoking*

-faire de l'exercice régulièrement: *exercise regularly*

-manger beaucoup de légumes *eat a lot of vegetables*

-manger sainement: *eat healthily*

-se reposer suffisamment: *have enough rest*

2. Ce que je mange *(what I eat)*

Je mange... *I eat...*

-des aliments sains: *healthy food*

-des épinards: *spinach*

-des fruits secs: *dried fruit*

-des haricots verts: *green beans*

-des œufs: *eggs*

3. Les boissons que je bois *(drinks I drink)*

Je bois: *I drink*

-de l'eau: *water*

-du jus de fruits: *fruit juice*

-du jus d'orange: *orange juice*

4. Les expressions de temps *(time)*

D'habitude: *Usually* / En général: *In general*

Tous les jours: *Every day*

5. Ce que je dois faire *(what I must do)*

Pour améliorer ma santé: *To improve my health*

Pour avoir de l'énergie: *To have energy*

Pour être en bonne santé: *To be in good health*

Pour rester en forme: *To stay in good shape*

6. Mes résolutions pour le futur

À l'avenir, j'ai l'intention d'... *In the future, I intend to...*

-arrêter de boire de l'alcool: *stop drinking alcohol*

-arrêter de fumer: *stop smoking*

Je vais faire un effort pour... *I'm going to make an effort to...*

-manger moins de sucreries: *eat less sugary foods*

-manger plus de légumes: *eat more vegetables*

7. Si je pouvais... *(If I could...)*

Si je pouvais... *If I could...*

-je cuisinerais plus moi-même *I would cook more myself*

1. Match up

Dormir	***To rest***
Éviter	***To stay***
Fumer	***To smoke***
Améliorer	***To sleep***
Rester	***To improve***
Arrêter	***To make an effort***
Faire un effort	***To cook***
Cuisiner	***To stop***
Se reposer	***To avoid***

2. Gapped translation

a. Je bois de l'eau: *I drink some* _________

b. Je mange des fruits secs: *I eat* _______ *fruit*

c. Pour rester en forme: *To stay in good* ________

d. En bonne santé: *In good* _________

e. Arrêter de fumer: *To stop* ___________

f. Je mange des œufs: *I eat some* _______

g. J'adore les haricots verts: *I love* ______ ______

h. J'aime les épinards: *I like* _____________

3. Broken words

a. San_ _

b. Alc_ _ _

c. Sucre_ _ _ _

d. Lég_ _ _ _

e. D'hab_ _ _ _ _

f. À l'ave_ _ _

g. Dor_ _ _

h. Des œu_ _

i. Des épi_ _ _ _ _

j. Des fr_ _ _ _ s_ _ _

k. De l'e_ _

l. Fu_ _ _

4. Complete with the missing words

a. Je bois ___ jus d'orange

b. Pour rester ___ forme

c. Tous ___ jours, je bois deux litres d'eau

d. J'ai _'intention _'arrêter de boire de l'alcool

e. Il faut __ reposer suffisamment

f. Je mange ___ aliments sains

g. Il faut dormir huit heures ___ nuit

h. Pour être ___ bonne santé

5. Translate into English

a. Les épinards:
b. Les sucreries:
c. Si je pouvais:
d. Santé:
e. Moi-même:
f. Les œufs:
g. L'eau:
h. Les légumes:
i. Fumer:
j. Des aliments sains:
k. Je cuisinerais:
l. J'ai l'intention de:

6. Missing vowels

a. L_s s_cr_r_ _s: *Sweets*
b. Il f_ _t: *It's necessary*
c. S_ j_ p_ _v_ _s: *If I could*
d. M_ _ns: *Less*
e. F_m_r: *To smoke*
f. _ l'_v_n_r: *In the future*

7. Anagrams

a. reriSuces
b. narÉpids
c. meruF
d. Dirorm
e. Aterrrê
f. Mnsoi
g. teResr
h. Satén

8. Sentence puzzle

a. santé, Pour en bonne il faut se rester suffisamment reposer
b. Si je je cuisinerais pouvais, moi-même plus
c. fruits jours, Tous les je beaucoup de et de légumes mange
d. d'arrêter À j'ai l'intention de fumer l'avenir,
e. rester aliments en forme, je des sains Pour mange
f. D'habitude, jus d'orange je bois du

9. Complete the table

English	Français
Spinach	
	Si je pouvais
To stop	
	Se reposer
To smoke	
	En bonne santé
To improve	
	Des aliment sains
To stay in shape	

10. Find in the wordsearch the French for the words listed in the box below

S	A	N	T	É	T	A
E	A	U	F	P	V	R
S	D	A	R	I	H	R
U	V	J	K	N	F	Ê
C	A	U	E	A	U	T
R	G	S	R	R	M	E
E	B	M	T	D	E	R
R	Z	O	Ê	S	R	G
I	N	I	N	L	U	T
E	A	N	Q	N	G	J
S	R	S	Y	I	E	P

To be:
Good:
Less:
To stop:
To smoke:
Health:
Spinach:
Water:
Juice:

11. Guided translation

a. E_ b______ s________ : *In good health*
b. S_j_ p___________: *If I could*
c. A_________ d_ f_______ : *To stop smoking*
d. P______ a_______________ : *To improve*
e. M__ s_________: *My health*
f. M_________ d___ s_____________ : *To eat sweets*
g. P____ a_______ d__ l'é___________ : *To have energy*
h. É_______ d__ b_______ d_ l'a_________ : *To avoid drinking alcohol*
i. Des h____________ v______ : *Green beans*
j. I_ f____ d________ : *It's necessary to sleep*

12. Translate into French

a. To stay in good health, I try to exercise regularly
b. I eat a lot of fruit and vegetables every day
c. I usually sleep eight hours a night and I always drink a lot of water
d. To stay in shape, I try to have enough rest
e. In the future, I am going to stop smoking
f. To have energy, I eat healthily
g. I am going to make an effort to eat less sweets
h. I am going to stop drinking fizzy drinks and alcohol
i. If I could, I would cook more myself at home
j. To improve my health, I am going to do more sport

UNIT 2 - Test (/100)

1. Vocabulary recognition: French-to-English gapped translation (/15)

a. En bonne santé: *In* _____ _______

b. J'essaye de dormir: *I* ____ *to* _______

c. Je devrais éviter: *I* ______ ________

d. Si j'avais: _____ *I* _____

e. Moins de sucreries: _____ _______

f. Je crois que: *I* ______ _______

g. Un régime équilibré: *A* _________ ________

h. Il faut manger: _______________ *to eat*

2. Syntax/Lexicogrammar – Split sentences (/5)

Si je	forme, je dois arrêter de fumer
Je crois	l'intention de faire plus de sport
Pour améliorer ma	pouvais, je cuisinerais plus souvent
À l'avenir, j'ai	manger plus de légumes
Je dois	que je suis en bonne forme

3. Grammar/Morphology/Vocabulary – Tangled translation (/20)

a. Je dois **stop** de **smoke**

b. Si j'**had** plus de **time**…

c. Je mange de la **food organic**

d. **Spinach** sont riches en **minerals**

e. **It is necessary to eat** assez de **vegetables**

f. Je **drink** beaucoup d'**water**

g. Je **must** arrêter de **drink** de l'**alcohol**

h. Pour **stay** en forme, je dois faire **more** de sport

i. Je **am going** faire un effort

j. Je mange beaucoup de produits **fresh**

4. Translate into French (/60 – each full sentence – 6 points)

a. I believe that I am in good shape

b. In order to improve my health, I must eat more fruit

c. If I could, I would do sport more regularly

d. I quite like eggs because they are rich in protein

e. In the future, I am going to avoid fried foods and sweets

f. If I had more time, I would do more cycling

g. I should avoid sweets and fatty foods

h. In order to have energy, I sleep eight hours per night

i. Generally, I have a balanced diet and I do enough sport

j. I don't eat sugar because it isn't healthy

Unit 2. Healthy/unhealthy living - Foundation - Answers

1. Match up (section 1)

Je dors – ***I sleep*** J'évite – ***I avoid*** Je ne mange pas – ***I don't eat*** Les fritures – ***Fried foods***
Je me détends – ***I relax*** Les matières grasses – ***Fat*** Sur mon ordinateur – ***On my computer***
Je sors – ***I go out*** Je fais de l'exercice – ***I exercise*** Un régime alimentaire – ***A diet***

2. Gapped translation (section 1)

a. J'évite les fritures: *I avoid* ***fried foods***
b. Je ne mange pas trop de matières grasses: *I don't eat too much* ***fat***
c. Je suis un régime alimentaire sain: *I follow a* ***healthy*** *diet*
d. Je mange cinq portions de fruits et légumes par jour: *I eat five portions of fruit and* ***vegetables*** *per day*
e. Je fais de l'exercice: *I* ***exercise***
f. Je me détends après l'école: *I* ***relax*** *after school*
g. Je ne prends pas de drogues: *I don't take* ***drugs***

3. Complete the sentences with a suitable verb, then translate them into English (Section 2)

a. Je **bois** beaucoup d'alcool: ***I drink a lot of alcohol***
b. Je **suis** toujours stressé: ***I am always stressed***
c. Je **mange** des sucreries: ***I eat sweets***
d. Je **fume** beaucoup de cigarettes: ***I smoke a lot of cigarettes***
e. Je **passe** beaucoup de temps sur les réseaux sociaux: ***I spend a lot of time on social media***
f. Je **bois** beaucoup de Coca et de Fanta: ***I drink a lot of Coke and Fanta***

4. Tick every sentence which refers to a healthy habit

a. Je bois beaucoup d'alcool b. Je passe huit heures par jour sur mon ordinateur
c. Je passe des heures sur les réseaux sociaux d. Je mange beaucoup de fritures et de sucreries
e. Je prends cinq portions de légumes par jour √ f. J'évite les fritures √

5. Complete the table (section 1)

I sleep eight hours per night: **Je dors huit heures par nuit** ***I relax***: Je me détends
I don't eat too much fat: Je ne mange pas trop de matières grasses
I follow a healthy diet: **Je suis un régime équilibré** ***I go out with my friends***: Je sors avec mes amis
I don't take any drugs: **Je ne prends pas de drogues**
I exercise regularly: **Je fais de l'exercice régulièrement** ***I avoid fried foods***: J'évite les fritures

6. Broken words (section 3)

a. S**ain**: *Healthy* b. Mal**sain**: *Unhealthy* c. Bo**n**: *Good* d. Noci**f** : *Harmful* e. Dan**gereux**: *Dangerous*
f. **Sucr**é: *Sweet* g. Mauv**ais**: *Bad* h. Équilibré: *Balanced* i. **Fati**gué: *Tired* j. Gr**as**: *Greasy*

7. Gapped English-to-French translation

a. Je **dors** huit heures par **nuit** b. Je ne **fume** pas **de** cigarettes c. J'évite les **fritures**
d. Je **passe** des **heures** sur les **réseaux sociaux** e. Je **fais** de l'exercice **régulièrement**
f. Les fritures sont **malsaines** g. Je mange cinq portions de **légumes** h. Je **sors** avec mes **amis**
i. Je **bois** beaucoup d'**alcool** j. Je ne **dors** pas **assez**

8. Spot and supply the one word missing in each sentence

a. Je **dors** huit heures par nuit b. Je ne **fume** pas de cigarettes c. Les fritures **sont** mauvaises pour la santé
d. Je passe beaucoup de temps sur les **réseaux** sociaux e. Je **suis** un régime alimentaire très sain
f. Je ne mange pas **de** sucreries

9. Guided translation

a. *Good*: **Bon** b. *Bad*: **Mauvais** c. *Healthy*: **Sain** d. *Greasy*: **Gras** e. *Harmful*: **Nocif** f. *Sweet*: **Sucré**
g. *Tired*: **Fatigué** h. *Drugs*: **Drogues** i. *Time*: **Temps** j. *Health*: **Santé**

10. Translate into French

a. Je dors au moins huit heures par nuit b. Je suis toujours fatigué(e) et stressé(e)
c. Je ne fume pas de cigarettes d. J'évite les fritures et les sucreries
e. Je passe des heures sur les réseaux sociaux et sur mon portable f. Je suis un régime alimentaire sain
g. Je fais de l'exercice régulièrement, mais je mange beaucoup de sucreries
h. Je ne prends pas de drogues, mais je fume parfois i. Je mange cinq portions de fruits et légumes par jour
j. Je ne bois pas de boissons gazeuses k. Les frites sont malsaines et grasses
l. Je passe une heure par jour sur internet

Unit 2. Healthy/unhealthy living - Higher - Answers

1. Match up

Dormir – ***To sleep*** Éviter – ***To avoid*** Fumer – ***To smoke*** Améliorer – ***To improve*** Rester – ***To stay***
Arrêter – ***To stop*** Faire un effort – ***To make an effort*** Cuisiner – ***To cook*** Se reposer – ***To rest***

2. Gapped translation

a. *I drink some* ***water*** b. *I eat* ***dried*** *fruit* c. *To stay in good* ***shape*** d. *In good* ***health***
e. *To stop* ***smoking*** f. *I eat some* ***eggs*** g. *I love* ***green beans*** h. *I like* ***spinach***

3. Broken words

a. Sant**é** b. Alc**ool** c. Sucre**ries** d. Lég**umes** e. D'hab**itude** f. À l'ave**nir** g. Dor**mir**
h. Des **œufs** i. Des épi**nards** j. Des fr**uits secs** k. De l'**eau** l. Fu**mer**

4. Complete with the missing words

a. Je bois **du** jus d'orange b. Pour rester **en** forme c. Tous **les** jours, je bois deux litres d'eau
d. J'ai **l'**intention **d'**arrêter de boire de l'alcool e. Il faut **se** reposer suffisamment
f. Je mange **des** aliments sains g. Il faut dormir huit heures **par** nuit h. Pour être **en** bonne santé

5. Translate into English

a. ***Spinach*** b. ***Sweets*** c. ***If I could*** d. ***Health*** e. ***Myself*** f. ***Eggs*** g. ***Water*** h. ***Vegetables***
i. ***To smoke*** j. ***Healthy food*** k. ***I would cook*** l. ***I intend to***

6. Missing vowels

a. **Les sucreries**: *Sweets* b. **Il faut**: *It's necessary* c. **Si je pouvais**: *If I could*
d. **Moins**: *Less* e. **Fumer**: *To smoke* f. **À l'avenir**: *In the future*

7. Anagrams

a. **Sucreries** b. **Épinards** c. **Fumer** d. **Dormir** e. **Arrêter** f. **Moins** g. **Rester** h. **Santé**

8. Sentence puzzle

a. Pour rester en bonne santé, il faut se reposer suffisamment b. Si je pouvais, je cuisinerais plus moi-même
c. Tous les jours, je mange beaucoup de fruits et de légumes d. À l'avenir, j'ai l'intention d'arrêter de fumer
e. Pour rester en forme, je mange des aliments sains f. D'habitude, je bois du jus d'orange

9. Complete the table

Spinach: **Épinards** ***If I could***: Si je pouvais *To stop*: **Arrêter** ***To rest***: Se reposer
To smoke: **Fumer** ***In good health***: En bonne santé *To improve*: **Améliorer**
Healthy food: Des aliment sains *To stay in shape*: **Rester en forme**

10. Find in the wordsearch the French for the words listed in the box below

To be: **Être** Good: **Bonne** Less: **Moins** To stop: **Arrêter** To smoke: **Fumer**
Health: **Santé** Spinach: **Épinards** Water: **Eau** Juice: **Jus**

11. Guided translation

a. **En bonne santé** b. **Si je pouvais** c. **Arrêter de fumer** d. **Pour améliorer** e. **Ma santé**
f. **Manger des sucreries** g. **Pour avoir de l'énergie** h. **Éviter de boire de l'alcool**
i. **Des haricots verts** j. **Il faut dormir**

12. Translate into French

a. Pour rester en bonne santé, j'essaye de faire de l'exercice régulièrement
b. Je mange beaucoup de fruits et (de) légumes tous les jours
c. D'habitude, je dors huit heures par nuit et je bois toujours beaucoup d'eau
d. Pour rester en forme, j'essaye de me reposer suffisamment
e. À l'avenir, je vais arrêter de fumer
f. Pour avoir de l'énergie, je mange sainement
g. Je vais faire un effort pour manger moins de sucreries
h. Je vais arrêter de boire des boissons gazeuses et de l'alcool
i. Si je pouvais, je cuisinerais plus moi-même à la maison/chez moi
j. Pour améliorer ma santé, je vais faire plus de sport

UNIT 2 - Test - Answers (/100)

1. Vocabulary recognition: French-to-English gapped translation (/15)

a. En bonne santé: *In **good health***

b. J'essaye de dormir: *I **try** to **sleep***

c. Je devrais éviter: *I **should avoid***

d. Si j'avais: ***If I had***

e. Moins de sucreries: ***Less sweets***

f. Je crois que: *I **believe that***

g. Un régime équilibré: *A **balanced diet***

h. Il faut manger: ***It's necessary** to eat **(1 point)***

2. Syntax/Lexicogrammar – Split sentences (/5)

Si je	**pouvais, je cuisinerais plus souvent**
Je crois	**que je suis en bonne forme**
Pour améliorer ma	**forme, je dois arrêter de fumer**
À l'avenir, j'ai	**l'intention de faire plus de sport**
Je dois	**manger plus de légumes**

3. Grammar/Morphology/Vocabulary – Tangled translation (/20)

a. Je dois **arrêter** de **fumer**

b. Si **j'avais** plus de **temps**…

c. Je mange de la **nourriture biologique**

d. **Les épinards** sont riches en **minéraux**

e. **Il faut manger** assez de **légumes**

f. Je **bois** beaucoup d'**eau**

g. Je **dois** arrêter de **boire** de l'**alcool**

h. Pour **rester** en forme, je dois faire **plus** de sport

i. Je **vais** faire un effort

j. Je mange beaucoup de produits **frais**

4. Translate into French (/60 – each full sentence – 6 points)

a. **Je crois que je suis en bonne forme**

b. **Pour améliorer ma santé, je dois manger plus de fruits**

c. **Si je pouvais, je ferais du sport plus régulièrement**

d. **J'aime assez les œufs parce qu' ils sont riches en protéines**

e. **À l'avenir, je vais éviter les fritures et les sucreries**

f. **Si j'avais plus de temps, je ferais plus de vélo**

g. **Je devrais éviter les sucreries et les aliments gras**

h. **Pour avoir de l'énergie, je dors huit heures par nuit**

i. **Généralement, j'ai un régime équilibré et je fais assez de sport**

j. **Je ne mange pas de (2) sucre parce que ce n'est pas sain**

Unit 3. Young people and fashion

KEY VOCABULARY Foundation

1. Les vêtements *(clothes)*

Des baskets: *Trainers*
Des chaussures: *Shoes*
Un haut: *A top*
Un pantalon: *Trousers*
Un pull: *A pullover*
Un short: *Shorts*
Une chemise: *A shirt*
Une jupe: *A skirt*
Une robe: *A dress*
Une veste: *A jacket*

2. Les couleurs *(colours)*

Blanc: *White* Bleu: *Blue*
Gris: *Grey* Jaune: *Yellow*
Noir: *Black* Rose: *Pink*
Vert: *Green*

3. Les accessoires *(accessories)*

Des boucles d'oreilles: *Earrings*
Un collier: *A necklace*
Un sac à dos: *A backpack*
Un sac à main: *A handbag*
Une casquette: *A cap*
Une montre: *A watch*

4. Les adjectifs importants

Beau/belle: *Beautiful*
Branché: *Trendy*
Cher/Chère: Expensive
Confortable: *Comfortable*
Démodé: *Unfashionable*
Moche: *Ugly*
Moulant: *Skin-tight*
Nouveau/nouvelle: *New*
Vieux/vieille: *Old*

5. Les expressions essentielles

À la mode: *Fashionable*
Bon marché: *Cheap*
Je porte: *I wear*
Je ne porte pas: *I don't wear*
J'aime: *I like*
Je n'aime pas: *I don't like*
Je préfère: *I prefer*
Les vêtements de marque: *Branded clothes*

1. Match up

Je porte un pantalon	***It's beautiful***
C'est beau	***I wear a dress***
Je porte une montre	***I wear a necklace***
Je porte une robe	***It's unfashionable***
C'est démodé	***I have a backpack***
J'ai un sac à dos	***I wear a watch***
Je porte une casquette	***I wear a top***
C'est nouveau	***I wear trousers***
Je porte une chemise	***It's new***
Je porte un haut	***I wear a shirt***
Je porte un collier	***It's trendy***
C'est branché	***I wear a cap***

2. Work out the colours and translate into English as shown in the example

a. Une robe **rigse**: Une robe **grise** - *A grey dress*
b. Un pull **ajeun**:
c. Un sac à dos **trev** et **roin**:
d. Une casquette **bulee**:
e. Une robe **ugero**:
f. Un short **clanb**:
g. Une chemise **oser**:

3. Circle the correct translation

a. Une montre: *a watch / a bracelet / a dress*
b. Une casquette: *a backpack / shorts / a cap*
c. Vieux: *new / old / nice*
d. Nouveau: *new / old / nice*
e. Branché: *ugly / trendy / old*
f. Moulant: *skin-tight / new / comfortable*
g. Un haut: *trousers / shorts / a top*

4. Complete the words and translate into English

a. Une nouv_ _ _ _ casqu_ _ _ _ : *A new cap*
b. Une mont_ _ à la mo_ _ : *A fashionable watch*
c. Une be_ _ _ ro_ _ rose: *A beautiful pink dress*
d. Des bouc_ _ _ d'oreilles ch_ _ _ _ : *Expensive earrings*
e. Je por_ _ un jean moul_ _ _ : *I am wearing skin-tight jeans*
f. Des _ _ _ _ ments de mar_ _ _ : *Branded clothes*
g. Une chem_ _ _ démo_ _ _ : *An unfashionable shirt*

5. Faulty translation – Correct the incorrect translations (Note: not all the translations are wrong)

a. Je porte une robe branchée: *I wear a trendy watch*

b. Elle porte une belle robe rose: *She wears a beautiful pink dress*

c. Il porte des vêtements de marque: *She wears branded clothes*

d. C'est une nouvelle casquette: *It's a new watch*

e. Ces chaussures sont vieilles: *These shoes are old*

f. Elle porte des vêtements bon marché: *They wear cheap clothes*

g. Je ne porte pas de jupes: *I don't wear skirts*

6. Missing vowels

a. _n_ r_b_ : *A dress*

b. D_s ch_ _ss_r_s: *Shoes*

c. _n c_ll_ _r: *A necklace*

d. _n_ m_ntr_ : *A watch*

e. _n s_c à m_ _n: *A handbag*

f. _n_ j_p_ : *A skirt*

g. _n s_c à d_s: *A backpack*

7. Translate into English

a. De belles chaussures à la mode

b. Une nouvelle casquette de marque

c. Une vieille robe noire

d. Une jupe verte démodée

e. Un beau collier branché

f. Une belle veste bleue

g. Des baskets branchées

8. Every adjective below needs correcting in order to agree with the noun in gender

a. Une beau robe: Une **belle** robe

b. Une nouveau montre: ________________

c. Une robe branché: ________________

d. Une vieux jupe: ________________

e. Une casquette demodé: ________________

f. Une beau chemise: ________________

g. Une nouveau veste: ________________

9. Sentences puzzles – rearrange the words in the correct order

a. porte vieille Je une montre marron
I wear an old brown watch

b. ne porte de Elle jupes pas
She doesn't wear skirts

c. Ta belle porte une mère robe
Your mother is wearing a beautiful dress

d. un demodé Mon pantalon père noir porte
My father is wearing black trousers

e. portons vêtements de marque des Nous
We wear branded clothes

f. ses nouvelles baskets Ma soeur porte
My sister is wearing her new trainers

10. Guided translation

a. A beautiful dress: *U__ b_______ r_______*

b. An old jacket: *U__ v________ v_______*

c. A new skirt: *U__ n___________ j________*

d. A trendy shirt: *U___ c___________ b__________*

e. A new necklace: *U__ n_________ c__________*

f. An unfashionable watch: *U__ m_______ d______*

g. A red handbag: *U_ s____ à m______ r__________*

11. Translate into French

a. I am wearing a pink top and black shoes

b. We are wearing our (*nos*) new white trainers

c. He is wearing a new cap

d. Usually, I wear a white shirt, blue jeans and black shoes

e. She is wearing a new watch, a new necklace and new earrings

f. My father wears unfashionable clothes

g. My mother is wearing an old yellow dress

h. My brother always wears trendy clothes

KEY VOCABULARY Higher

1. C'est quoi la mode? ***What is fashion?***

L'allure/Le look: *Look*
L'apparence: *Appearance*
La mode: *Fashion*
Le maquillage: *Make-up*
Le style vestimentaire: *Clothing style*
Les accessoires: *Accessories*
Les bijoux: *Jewellery*
Les marques: *Brands*
Les robes: *Dresses*
Les sacs à main: *Handbags*
Les tatouages: *Tattoos*
Les vêtements: *Clothes*

2. Pourquoi la mode est importante?

Les jeunes portent des vêtements de marque
Young people wear branded clothes
Beaucoup de jeunes portent des vêtements à la mode
Many young people wear fashionable clothes
C'est un moyen/une manière… *It's a means/way…*
-d'attirer les garçons/les filles
to attract boys/girls
-de plaire aux autres: *to appeal to others*
-de s'intégrer dans un groupe *to fit in a group*

La mode permet de… *Fashion allows one to…*
-se faire remarquer: *get noticed*
-s'exprimer: *express oneself*

La plupart des adolescents s'habillent pour impressionner
Most adolescents dress to impress
Les accessoires aident à… *Accessories help to…*
-définir son identité: *define one's identity*
-améliorer son image: *improve one's image*
-se démarquer: *stand out*

3. Les points négatifs de la mode

Cela coûte cher: *It costs dearly*
Cela met de la pression sur les adolescents:
It puts some pressure on adolescents
Cela peut devenir une addiction:
It can become an addiction
Cela nous encourage au gaspillage d'argent et de matériaux: *It encourages us to the waste of money and materials*

4. Les verbes importants

Porter: *To wear*
S'habiller: *To get dressed*
Se maquiller: *To put make-up on*

1. Match up (section 1)

Porter	***Clothes***
L'allure	***Brands***
La mode	***Dresses***
Les vêtements	***Fashion***
Les bijoux	***Handbags***
Les marques	***Look***
Les sacs à main	***Jewellery***
Se maquiller	***To put make-up on***
Les robes	***To wear***

2. Faulty translation (section 2): correct the wrong translations

a. La plupart des jeunes: *Some young people*
b. Se faire remarquer: *To be accepted*
c. Améliorer: *To wear*
d. Plaire aux autres: *To appeal to others*
e. Des vêtements de marque: *Branded clothes*
f. Les jeunes s'habillent: *Young people like*
g. À la mode: *Fashionable*

3. Broken words (section 1)

a. Le maqui_ _ _ _ _
b. Les sacs à m_ _ _
c. Les bij_ _ _
d. La mo_ _
e. L'all_ _ _
f. Les tatou_ _ _ _
g. Por_ _ _
h. Pl_ _ _ _ aux autres
i. Les mar_ _ _ _
j. Les access_ _ _ _ _
k. Les rob_ _
l. S'habi_ _ _ _

4. Complete with the missing words (sections 2 & 3)

a. Beaucoup de _______ : *Many young people*
b. Les accessoires ________ : *Accessories help*
c. Cela peut ___________ : *It can become*
d. Se ______________ : *To stand out*
e. ________ les filles: *To attract girls*
f. C'est un ________ de: *It is a means to*
g. ________ aux autres: *To appeal to others*
h. Cela ____ de la pression: *It puts some pressure*

5. Translate into English

a. La mode:

b. Cela peut devenir:

c. Se démarquer:

d. Attirer les garçons:

e. Se faire remarquer:

f. Les bijoux:

g. C'est un moyen:

h. Le gaspillage:

i. La mode:

j. Améliorer son look:

k. L'allure:

l. À la mode:

6. Missing vowels (section 3)

a. L_ g_sp_ll_g_ : *Waste*

b. Ch_r: *Dear(ly)*

c. D_v_n_r: *To become*

d. _rg_nt: *Money*

e. C_l_ m_t: *It puts*

f. C_l_ c_ _t_ : *It costs*

7. Anagrams (section 1)

a. uxBioj

b. deMo

c. Vêntsteme

d. bilS'haler

e. ouTatages

f. luAlre

g. rqMaues

h. cessoAcires

8. Sentence puzzle

a. accessoires Les aident à son definir identité

b. moyen C'est un de autres aux plaire

c. Cela encourage nous au d'argent gaspillage

d. se Les permettent de démarquer tatouages

e. devenir Cela addiction peut une

f. coûte La cher mode

g. image La à mode aide améliorer son

9. Complete the table

English	Français
Jewellery	
	Allure
	Cela peut devenir
To get dressed	
Tattoos	
	Améliorer son image
	Un moyen de plaire
Others	
	S'exprimer

10. Find in the wordsearch the French for the words listed in the box below

S	A	L	L	U	R	E
E	U	G	M	O	D	E
M	T	N	U	Q	À	V
O	R	L	O	P	L	X
Y	E	Z	F	K	A	P
E	S	E	C	P	M	O
N	D	É	I	H	O	R
A	H	U	A	B	D	T
P	L	A	I	R	E	E
D	E	V	E	N	I	R
O	C	O	Û	T	E	T

Look: A

Fashionable: À

Others: A

Fashion: M

To become: D

To wear: P

(It) costs: C

To appeal: P

Means: M

11. Guided translation

a. *Fashion costs dearly*: L_ m_ _ _ c_ _ _ _ c_ _ _

b. *To appeal to others*: P_ _ _ _ _ a_ _ a_ _ _ _ _

c. *To wear jewellery*: P_ _ _ _ _ d_ _ b_ _ _ _ _

d. *It allows to express oneself*:
Ça p_ _ _ _ _ d_ s' e_ _ _ _ _ _ _

e. *Branded clothes*: D_ _ v_ _ _ _ _ _ _ _ _ d_ m_ _ _ _ _

f. *To improve one's image*:A_ _ _ _ _ _ _ _ s_ _ i_ _ _ _

g. *To get noticed*: S_ f_ _ _ _ r_ _ _ _ _ _ _ _ _

h. *Some pressure*: D_ l_ p_ _ _ _ _ _ _

i. *It can become*: C_ _ _ p_ _ _ d_ _ _ _ _ _

12. Translate into French

a. Fashion can become an addiction

b. Many young people wear branded clothes

c. Fashion allows adolescents to stand out

d. Tattoos allow one to get noticed

e. Fashion is a means to attract boys

f. Sadly, it encourages us to the waste of money

g. Clothes allow us to improve our image

h. Fashion costs dearly

UNIT 3 - Test (/100)

1. Vocabulary recognition: French-to-English translation (/15)

a. Actuellement:
b. Attirer:
c. La mode:
d. Dernières:
e. De nos jours:
f. Vêtements:
g. Marque:
h. Il faut:
i. Bijoux:
j. Allure:
k. Jeunes (noun):
i. Moqueries:
j. Laisser:
k. Chaussures:
l. Plaire :

2. Syntax/Lexicogrammar – Split sentences (/5)

Je suis les dernières	pas la mode
Les vêtements aident	la mode peut encourager les moqueries
Personnellement, je n'aime	tendances de la mode
Ce qui est triste, c'est que	à s'exprimer
Le look est un moyen de	se démarquer des autres

3. Grammar/Morphology/Vocabulary – Tangled translation (/20)

a. J'aime porter des **pretty dresses** roses
b. Je ne **wear** pas de vêtements de **brand**
c. Je ne **follow** pas la **fashion**
d. J'adore les **jewellery** et les **tattoos**
e. Le look est une **way** d'**attract** les filles
f. **It's** un **means** de **express oneself**
g. **Most** jeunes s'habillent pour **impress**
h. Les accessoires **help** à se démarquer des **others**
i. Cela **can become** une addiction
j. Le look les aide à **fit in** un groupe

4. Translate into French (/ 60 – each full sentence – 6 points)

a. Fashion can become an addiction for many young people
b. Fashion is a way to define one's identity
c. Nowadays, many adolescents have branded bags
d. I don't wear jewellery, but I have tattoos
e. Clothes help us to improve our image
f. For many young people, clothing style is very important
g. It is a way to get noticed by others
h. I don't follow fashion because it is too expensive
i. Accessories help us stand out from others
j. We must let young people develop their own identity

Unit 3. Young people and fashion - Foundation - Answers

1. Match up

Je porte un pantalon – ***I wear trousers*** C'est beau – ***It's beautiful*** Je porte une montre – ***I wear a watch***
Je porte une robe – ***I wear a dress*** C'est démodé – ***It's unfashionable***
J'ai un sac à dos – ***I have a backpack*** Je porte une casquette – ***I wear a cap*** C'est nouveau – ***It's new***
Je porte une chemise – ***I wear a shirt*** Je porte un haut – ***I wear a top***
Je porte un collier – ***I wear a necklace*** C'est branché – ***It's trendy***

2. Work out the colours and translate into English as shown in the example

a. Une robe **rigse**: Une robe **grise** - *A grey dress* b. Un pull **ajeun**: Un pull **jaune** - ***A yellow pullover***
c. Un sac à dos **trev** et **roin**: Un sac à dos **vert** et **noir** - ***A green and black backpack***
d. Une casquette **bulee**: Une casquette **bleue** - ***A blue cap*** e. Une robe **ugero**: Une robe **rouge** - ***A red dress***
f. Un short **clanb**: Un short **blanc** - ***White shorts*** g. Une chemise **oser**: Une chemise **rose** - ***A pink shirt***

3. Circle the correct translation

a. Une montre: ***a watch*** b. Une casquette: ***a cap*** c. Vieux: ***old*** d. Nouveau: ***new***
e. Branché: ***trendy*** f. Moulant: ***skin-tight*** g. Un haut: ***a top***

4. Complete the words and translate into English

a. Une nouv**elle** casque**tte**: *A new cap* b. Une mont**re** à la mo**de**: *A fashionable watch*
c. Une be**lle** ro**be** rose: *A beautiful pink dress* d. Des boucl**es** d'oreilles ch**è**res: *Expensive earrings*
e. Je por**te** un jean moul**ant**: *I am wearing skin-tight jeans* f. Des **vête**ments de mar**que**: *Branded clothes*
g. Une chemi**se** démo**dée**: *An unfashionable shirt*

5. Faulty translation – Correct the incorrect translations – (Note: not all the translations are wrong)

a. *I wear a trendy **dress*** b. Elle porte une belle robe rose √ c. ***He** wears branded clothes*
d. *It's a new **cap*** e. *These shoes are old* √ f. ***She wears** cheap clothes* g. *I don't wear skirts* √

6. Missing vowels

a. **Une robe**: *A dress* b. **Des chaussures**: *Shoes* c. **Un collier**: *A necklace* d. **Une montre**: *A watch*
e. **Un sac à main**: *A handbag* f. **Une jupe**: *A skirt* g. **Un sac à dos**: *A backpack*

7. Translate into English

a. ***Beautiful fashionable shoes*** b. ***A new branded cap*** c. ***An old black dress***
d. ***An unfashionable green skirt*** e. ***A beautiful trendy necklace*** f. ***A beautiful blue jacket***
g. ***Trendy trainers***

8. Every adjective below needs correcting in order to agree with the noun in gender

a. Une beau robe: Une **belle** robe b. Une nouveau montre: Une **nouvelle** montre
c. Une robe branché: Une robe **branchée** d. Une vieux jupe: Une **vieille** jupe
e. Une casquette demodé: Une casquette **démodée** f. Une beau chemise: Une **belle** chemise
g. Une nouveau veste: Une **nouvelle** veste

9. Sentences puzzles – rearrange the words in the correct order

a. **Je porte une vieille montre marron** b. **Elle ne porte pas de jupes** c. **Ta mère porte une belle robe**
d. **Mon père porte un pantalon noir demodé** e. **Nous portons des vêtements de marque**
f. **Ma soeur porte ses nouvelles baskets**

10. Guided translation

a. **Une belle robe** b. **Une vieille veste** c. **Une nouvelle jupe** d. **Une chemise branchée**
e. **Un nouveau collier** f. **Une montre démodée** g. **Un sac à main rouge**

11. Translate into French

a. **Je porte un haut rose et des chaussures noires** b. **Nous portons nos nouvelles baskets blanches**
c. **Il porte une nouvelle casquette**
d. **D'habitude, je porte une chemise blanche, un jean bleu et des chaussures noires**
e. **Elle porte une nouvelle montre, un nouveau collier et des nouvelles boucles d'oreilles**
f. **Mon père porte des vêtements démodés** g. **Ma mère porte une vieille robe jaune**
h. **Mon frère porte toujours des vêtements branchés**

Unit 3. Young people and fashion - Higher - Answers

1. Match up (section 1)

Porter – ***To wear*** L'allure – ***Look*** La mode – ***Fashion*** Les vêtements – ***Clothes***
Les bijoux – ***Jewellery*** Les marques – ***Brands*** Les sacs à main – ***Handbags***
Se maquiller – ***To put make-up on*** Les robes – ***Dresses***

2. Faulty translation (section 2): correct the wrong translations

a. ***Most** young people* b. *To **get noticed*** c. *To **improve*** d. *To appeal to others* √ e. *Branded clothes* √
f. *Young people **dress*** g. *Fashionable* √

3. Broken words (section 1)

a. Le maqui**llage** b. Les sacs à m**ain** c. Les bij**oux** d. La mo**de** e. L'all**ure** f. Les tatou**ages**
g. Por**ter** h. Pl**aire** aux autres i. Les mar**ques** j. Les access**oires** k. Les rob**es** l. S'habi**ller**

4. Complete with the missing words (sections 2 & 3)

a. Beaucoup de **jeunes** b. Les accessoires **aident** c. Cela peut **devenir** d. Se **démarquer**
e. **Attirer** les filles f. C'est un **moyen** de g. **Plaire** aux autres h. Cela **met** de la pression

5. Translate into English

a. **Fashion** b. **It can become** c. **To stand out** d. **To attract boys** e. **To get noticed** f. **Jewellery**
g. **It's a means** h. **Waste** i. **Fashion** j. **To improve one's look** k. **The look** l. **Fashionable**

6. Missing vowels (Section 3)

a. **Le gaspillage** b. **Cher** c. **Devenir** d. **Argent** e. **Cela met** f. **Cela coûte**

7. Anagrams (Section 1)

a. **Bijoux** b. **Mode** c. **Vêtements** d. **S'habiller** e. **Tatouages** f. **Allure** g. **Marques** h. **Accessoires**

8. Sentence puzzle

a. Les accessoires aident à definir son identité b. C'est un moyen de plaire aux autres
c. Cela nous encourage au gaspillage d'argent d. Les tatouages permettent de se démarquer
e. Cela peut devenir une addiction f. La mode coûte cher g. La mode aide à améliorer son image

9. Complete the table

Jewellery: **Bijoux** *Look*: Allure ***It can become***: Cela peut devenir *To get dressed*: **S'habiller**
Tattoos: **Tatouages** ***To improve one's image***: Améliorer son image
A means to appeal: Un moyen de plaire *Others*: **Autres** ***To express oneself***: S'exprimer

10. Find in the wordsearch the French for the words listed in the box below

Look: **Allure** *Fashionable*: **À la mode** *Others*: **Autres** *Fashion*: **Mode** *To become*: **Devenir**
To wear: **Porter** *(It) costs*: **Coûte** *To appeal*: **Plaire** *Means*: **Moyen**

11. Guided translation

a. **La mode coûte cher** b. **Plaire aux autres** c. **Porter des bijoux** d. **Ça permet de s'exprimer**
e. **Des vêtements de marque** f. **Améliorer son image** g. **Se faire remarquer** h. **De la pression**
i. **Cela peut devenir**

12. Translate into French

a. **La mode peut devenir une addiction**
b. **Beaucoup de jeunes portent des vêtements de marque**
c. **La mode permet aux adolescents de se démarquer**
d. **Les tatouages permettent de se faire remarquer**
e. **La mode est un moyen d'attirer les garçons**
f. **Malheureusement, cela encourage le gaspillage d'argent**
g. **Les vêtements nous permettent d'améliorer notre image**
h. **La mode coûte cher**

UNIT 3 - Test - Answers (/100)

1. Vocabulary recognition: French-to-English translation (/15)

a. Actuellement: ***Currently***

b. Attirer: ***To attract***

c. La mode: ***Fashion***

d. Dernières: ***Latest***

e. De nos jours: ***Nowadays***

f. Vêtements: ***Clothes***

g. Marque: ***Brand***

h. Il faut: ***It's necessary to***

i. Bijoux: ***Jewellery***

j. Allure: ***Look***

k. Jeunes (noun): ***Young people***

i. Moqueries: ***Mocking***

j. Laisser: ***To let***

k. Chaussures: ***Shoes***

l. Plaire: ***To appeal***

2. Syntax/Lexicogrammar – Split sentences (/5)

Je suis les dernières	**tendances de la mode**
Les vêtements aident	**à s'exprimer**
Personnellement, je n'aime	**pas la mode**
Ce qui est triste, c'est que	**la mode peut encourager les moqueries**
Le look est un moyen de	**se démarquer des autres**

3. Grammar/Morphology/Vocabulary – Tangled translation (/20)

a. J'aime porter de **belles robes** roses

b. Je ne **porte** pas de vêtements de **marque**

c. Je ne **suis** pas la **mode**

d. J'adore les **bijoux** et les **tatouages**

e. Le look est une **manière** d'**attirer** les filles

f. **C'est** un **moyen** de **s'exprimer**

g. **La plupart des** jeunes s'habillent pour **impressionner**

h. Les accessoires **aident** à se démarquer des **autres**

i. Cela **peut devenir** une addiction

j. Le look les aide à **s'intégrer dans** un groupe

4. Translate into French (/ 60 – each full sentence – 6 points)

a. **La mode peut devenir une addiction pour beaucoup de jeunes**

b. **La mode est une manière de définir son identité**

c. **De nos jours, beaucoup d' adolescents ont des sacs de marque**

d. **Je ne porte pas de (2) bijoux, mais j'ai des tatouages**

e. **Les vêtements nous aident à améliorer notre image**

f. **Pour beaucoup de jeunes, le style vestimentaire est très important**

g. **C'est une manière de se faire remarquer (2) par les autres**

h. **Je ne suis pas la mode parce que c'est trop cher**

i. **Les accessoires nous aident à nous démarquer des autres**

j. **Nous devons laisser les jeunes développer leur propre identité**

Unit 4. Environment: global problems

KEY VOCABULARY Foundation

1. Les activités polluantes

La déforestation: *Deforestation*

Le rejet d'eaux usées *The release of wastewater*

L'élevage intensif: *Intensive farming*

L'utilisation de produits chimiques *The use of chemical products*

L'utilisation de pesticides *The use of pesticides*

Les combustibles fossiles *Fossil fuels*

Les déchets industriels *Industrial waste*

Les embouteillages: *Traffic jams*

Les gaz d'échappement *Exhaust gases*

Les transports: *Transports*

Les usines: *Factories*

2. Les animaux en danger

Les baleines bleues: *Blue whales*

Les orang-outangs: *Orangutans*

Les ours polaires: *Polar bears*

3. Les problèmes

La fonte des glaces *The melting of the ice caps*

La montée du niveau de la mer *The sea level rise*

La sécheresse: *Drought*

La surconsommation *Overconsumption*

Le réchauffement climatique *Global warming*

L'augmentation de la population *The population increase*

L'effet de serre *The greenhouse effect*

Les feux de forêts: *Forest fires*

Les inondations: *Floods*

4. Les adjectifs utiles *(useful)*

Artificiel: *Artificial*

Naturel: *Natural*

5. Les verbes importants

Augmenter: *To increase*

Causer: *To cause*

Consommer: *To consume*

Contribuer: *To contribute*

Menacer: *To threaten*

Mettre en danger: *To endanger*

Protéger: *To protect*

1. Match up

Les ours	***Industrial waste***
L'élevage intensif	***Bears***
Les produits chimiques	***Traffic jams***
Les déchets industriels	***Blue whales***
Les eaux usées	***Chemical products***
Les baleines bleues	***Intensive farming***
Les usines	***Release***
Le rejet	***Wastewater***
Les embouteillages	***Factories***

2. Spot and fix the incorrect translations (sections 1 & 2)

a. Les déchets industriels: *Industrial developments*

b. Les baleines bleues: *Blue birds*

c. Les usines: *Public transport*

d. L'élevage intensif: *Intense traffic*

e. Les embouteillages: *Bottles*

f. Le rejet d'eaux usées: *The release of chemical waste*

g. Les gaz d'échappement: *Exhaust gases*

3. Gapped translation (section 3)

a. L'effet de serre: *The* _______________ *effect*

b. La montée du niveau de la mer: *The* _____ ________ *rise*

c. Les inondations fréquentes: *The frequent* _____________

d. La surconsommation de nourriture: *The* __________________ *of food*

e. L'augmentation de la population: *The population* _________

f. Les feux de forêts: *Forest* __________

g. La fonte des glaces: *The* ___________ *of the ice caps*

4. Translate into English

a. Effet de serre

b. Menacer

c. Sécheresses

d. Feux

e. Inondations

f. Baleines

g. Déchets

h. Embouteillages

i. Ours

j. Produits

k. Gaz

l. Eaux usées

m. Niveau

n. Usines

5. Complete and translate the phrases into English

a. Les séche_ _ _ _ _ _ :

b. Le réchau_ _ _ _ _ _ _ climatique:

c. L'augme_ _ _ _ _ _ _ de la population:

d. La _ _forestation:

e. Les dé_ _ _ _ _ industriels:

f. La mon_ _ _ du niveau de la mer:

g. Les ou_ _ polaires:

h. Les fe_ _ de forêts:

6. Break the flow

a. Lamontéeduniveaudelamer

b. Lafontedesglaces

c. Lesbaleinesbleues

d. Lesfeuxdeforêts

e. Laugmentationdelapopulation

f. Lerejetdeauxusées

g. Lutilisationdesproduitschimiques

h. Lutilisationdespesticides

7. Missing vowels

a. L_ d_f_r_st_t_ _n

b. L_s _s_n_s

c. L_s b_l_ _n_s bl_ _ _s

d. L_s d_ch_ts _nd_str_ _ls

e. L_ r_ch_ _ff_m_nt cl_m_t_qu_

f. L_ r_j_t d'_ _ _x _s_ _s

g. L_s s_ch_r_ss_s

h. L_ f_nt_ d_s gl_c_s

8. Find in the wordsearch the French for the words listed in the box below

S	É	C	H	E	R	E	S	S	E
A	E	T	U	O	S	Q	Z	Y	L
T	O	R	F	T	E	A	U	X	M
I	U	O	E	Y	Q	I	P	N	V
F	R	X	U	S	I	N	E	S	A
O	S	C	X	R	U	E	T	P	P
N	U	G	L	F	S	V	N	C	M
T	D	É	C	H	E	T	S	T	R
E	A	J	D	L	Y	E	Q	R	S

Drought: S
Bear: O
Fires: F
Waters: E
Factories: U
Waste: D
Melting: F

9. Supply the missing word

a. La ________ des glaces: *The melting of the ice caps*

b. La _________ du niveau de la mer: *The sea level rise*

c. Le rejet d' _______ usées: *The release of wastewater*

d. Les __________ industriels: *Industrial waste*

e. L'_________ de la population: *The population increase*

f. Les __________ bleues: *Blue whales*

g. ______ les espèces animales: *To threaten animal species*

10. Translate into French

a. *Droughts*: S

b. *Release*: R

c. *Waste*: D

d. *To threaten*: M

e. *Warming*: R

f. *Increase*: A

g. *Melting*: F

h. *Waters*: E

i. *Traffic jams*: E

j. *Level*: N

k. *Sea*: M

l. *Effect*: E

m. *Greenhouse*: S

n. *Factories*: U

11. English to French translation

a. The use of chemical products

b. Intensive farming

c. Global warming

d. The overconsumption of food

e. Industrial waste

f. The release of wastewater

g. Traffic jams contribute to air pollution

h. Fossil fuels contribute to greenhouse effect and global warming

i. The melting of the ice caps causes the sea level rise

j. Blue whales and polar bears are endangered animals

k. The increase in world population contributes to the exhaustion of natural resources

KEY VOCABULARY Higher

1. Les problèmes mondiaux *(global issues)*

L'effet de serre: *The greenhouse effect*

La disparition d'espèces animales

The extinction of animal species

La disparition d'espèces végétales

The extinction of plant species

L'épuisement des ressources naturelles

The exhaustion of natural resources

La fonte des glaces: *The melting of the ice caps*

La montée du niveau de la mer: *The sea level rise*

La pollution de l'air: *Air pollution*

La pollution de l'eau: *Water pollution*

La pollution des sols: *Soil pollution*

Le gaspillage de nourriture: *Food waste*

La pénurie de denrées alimentaires

The shortage of foodstuffs

Le réchauffement climatique: *Global warming*

Les inondations: *Floods*

2. Les causes

L'agriculture: *Agriculture*

L'augmentation de la population mondiale

The world population increase

L'espèce humaine: *The human species*

L'industrie: *The industry*

La chasse: *Hunting*

La déforestation: *Deforestation*

La surconsommation: *Overconsumption*

Le trafic aérien: *Air traffic*

Le trafic routier: *Road traffic*

Le transport aérien: *Air transport*

Les combustibles fossiles: *Fossil fuels*

Les gaz à effet de serre: *Greenhouse gases*

3. Les verbes importants

Arrêter: *To stop*

Être causé par: *To be caused by*

Jouer un rôle: *To play a role*

Menacer: *To threaten*

Mettre en danger: *To endanger*

Rendre (visible): *To make (visible)*

1. Match up (section 1)

Floods	L'effet de serre
Greenhouse effect	Les espèces animales
The rise	Les inondations
Soils	La fonte des glaces
Melting of the ice caps	La montée
Warming	Le niveau de la mer
Sea level	La disparition
Animal species	Les sols
Extinction	Le réchauffement

2. Gapped phrases (sections 1 & 2) – Complete and translate

a. Le ____________ de nourriture:

b. L'__________ humaine:

c. Le ___________ aérien:

d. La pollution de l'_______ et de l'______ :

e. Les gaz à effet de ________ :

f. La ________ du niveau de la mer:

3. Broken words (sections 2 & 3)

a. Les inonda_ _ _ _ _	g. La cha_ _ _
b. Les ga_	h. Rout_ _ _
c. Le gaspi_ _ _ _ _	i. La dispa_ _ _ _ _ _
d. Les combust_ _ _ _ _	j. Aér_ _ _
e. Le niv_ _ _	k. La nourri_ _ _ _
f. La mon_ _ _	l. La pén_ _ _ _

4. Faulty translation – Correct the wrong translations (sections 2 & 3)

a. Mettre en danger: *To preserve*

b. Le trafic routier: *Air traffic*

c. Jouer un rôle: *To play a role*

d. Rendre visible: *To make visible*

e. Arrêter: *To start*

f. La chasse: *Fishing*

g. Menacer: *To protect*

5. Translate into English

a. Le trafic routier
b. La chasse
c. Les combustibles
d. La montée
e. L'effet de serre
f. La surconsommation
g. Le réchauffement climatique
h. L'espèce
i. Mondiale
j. S'arrêter
k. L'épuisement
l. Mettre en danger

6. Missing vowels

a. L'_sp_c_
b. L_ ch_ss_
c. Ép_ _s_m_nt
d. L_s c_mb_st_bl_s
e. L_ tr_f_c r_ _t_ _r
f. L_ r_ch_ _ff_m_nt

7. Anagrams

a. cesèEsp
b. eauvNi
c. asChse
d. entiseÉpum
e. Comblesbusti
f. teFon
g. acesGl
h. Rchéamentuffe

8. Sentence puzzle

a. d'augmenter mondiale La population pas n'arrête
b. humaines L'effet serre de est par les activités augmenté
c. en plus humaine L'espèce impose de plus sa présence le paysage dans
d. inondations La mer des glaces provoque des en bord de fonte
e. d'espèces La disparition faune animales la diversité de la menace
f. température La des de s'accroître océans continue

9. Complete the table

English	Français
Hunting	
	Épuisement
Global warming	
Fuels	
	Gaspillage
Melting	
	Inondations
To increase	
	Disparition

10. Find in the wordsearch the French for the words listed in the box below

S	I	R	É	T	I	P
P	N	C	P	D	A	E
É	O	B	U	I	I	S
N	N	J	I	V	R	S
U	D	E	S	E	H	A
R	A	C	E	R	F	H
I	T	È	M	S	A	C
E	I	P	E	I	U	E
X	O	S	N	T	N	A
A	N	E	T	É	E	U
F	O	N	T	E	C	B

Hunting:
Fauna:
Diversity:
Exhaustion:
Species:
Flood:
Shortage:
Water:
Air:
Melting:

11. Guided translation

a. *Melting of the ice caps*:
L_ f________ d__ g______
b. *The extinction of animal species*:
L_ d_________ d'e_________ a__________
c. *Greenhouse gases*:
L__ g___ à e______ d_ s______
d. *The exhaustion of natural resources*:
L'é_________ d___ r__________ n__________
e. *Global warming*:
L__ r________________ c__________
f. *The ocean temperature*:
L_ t_________________ d___ o__________
g. *World population*: L_ p__________ m__________

12. Translate into French

a. The melting of the ice caps
b. The activities of the human species
c. The extinction of animal and plant species
d. The sea level rise
e. Global warming is a worrying phenomenon
f. Air pollution threatens our health
g. Floods are more and more frequent
h. There is a lot of waste of natural resources
i. Road traffic is responsible for the emission of greenhouse gases
j. The use of pesticides causes water pollution

UNIT 4 - Test (/100)

1. Vocabulary recognition: French-to-English translation (/15)

a. La fonte des glaces

b. Les usines

c. L'effet de serre

d. Les déchets

e. Les embouteillages

f. Menacer

g. Les feux

h. La sécheresse

i. La disparition

j. La mer

k. Le paysage

l. La pénurie

m. Les inondations

n. Les combustibles

o. La surconsommation

2. Syntax/Lexicogrammar – Split sentences (/5)

La population mondiale n'arrête	par les activités humaines
La fonte des glaces provoque	est accéléré par la pollution
L'effet de serre est accéléré	pas d'augmenter
Le réchauffement climatique	des ressources
Il faut réduire le gaspillage	la montée du niveau de la mer

3. Grammar/Morphology/Vocabulary – Tangled translation (/20)

a. Les **gases** d'échappement des **cars**

b. La **melting** des **ice caps**

c. La **extinction** des **species** animales

d. **There are** des **traffic jams**

e. L'**increase** de la population

f. L'**exhaustion** des ressources naturelles

g. **In** les zones **coastal**

h. Le **waste** de **food**

i. Son **footprint** sur l'**environment**

j. La **rise** du **level** de la mer

k. Les **fuels** fossiles

l. Le **warming** climatique

4. Translate into French (/ 60 – each full sentence – 6 points)

a. Fossil fuels contribute to the greenhouse effect

b. The melting of the ice caps causes the sea level rise

c. Blue whales and polar bears are endangered species

d. Traffic jams are an important cause of air pollution

e. The population increase is the main cause of pollution

f. Deforestation is one of the causes of global warming

g. The ocean temperature keeps growing every day

h. The sea level rise causes floods at the seaside

i. The greenhouse effect is accelerated by pollution

j. Overconsumption plays an important role in the exhaustion of natural resources

Unit 4. Environment: global problems - Foundation - Answers

1. Match up

Les ours – ***Bears*** L'élevage intensif – ***Intensive farming*** Les produits chimiques – ***Chemical products***
Les déchets industriels – ***Industrial waste*** Les eaux usées – ***Wastewater*** Les baleines bleues – ***Blue whales***
Les usines – ***Factories*** Le rejet – ***Release*** Les embouteillages – ***Traffic jams***

2. Spot and fix the incorrect translations (Sections 1 & 2)

a. *Industrial **waste*** b. *Blue **whales*** c. ***Factories*** d. ***Intensive farming*** e. ***Traffic jams***
f. *The release of **wastewater*** g. *Exhaust gases* √

3. Gapped translation (Section 3)

a. *The **greenhouse** effect* b. *The **sea level** rise* c. *The frequent **floods*** d. *The **overconsumption** of food*
e. *The population **increase*** f. *Forest **fires*** g. *The **melting** of the ice caps*

4. Translate into English

a. ***Greenhouse effect*** b. ***To threaten*** c. ***Droughts*** d. ***Fires*** e. ***Floods*** f. ***Whales*** g. ***Waste***
h. ***Traffic jams*** i. ***Bears*** j. ***Products*** k. ***Gas(es)*** l. ***Wastewater*** m. ***Level*** n. ***Factories***

5. Complete and translate the phrases into English

a. Les séche**resses**: ***Droughts*** b. Le récha**uffement** climatique: ***Global warming***
c. L'augme**ntation** de la population: ***The population increase*** d. La **dé**forestation: ***Deforestation***
e. Les dé**chets** industriels: ***Industrial waste*** f. La mont**ée** du niveau de la mer: ***The sea level rise***
g. Les ou**rs** polaires: ***Polar bears*** h. Les fe**ux** de forêts: ***Forest fires***

6. Break the flow

a. La montée du niveau de la mer b. La fonte des glaces c. Les baleines bleues d. Les feux de forêts
e. L'augmentation de la population f. Le rejet d'eaux usées g. L'utilisation des produits chimiques
h. L'utilisation des pesticides

7. Missing vowels

a. **La déforestation** b. **Les usines** c. **Les baleines bleues** d. **Les déchets industriels**
e. **Le réchauffement climatique** f. **Le rejet d'eaux usées** g. **Les sécheresses** h. **La fonte des glaces**

8. Find in the wordsearch the French for the words listed in the box below

Drought: **Sécheresse** Bear: **Ours** Fires: **Feux** Waters: **Eaux** Factories: **Usines**

Waste: **Déchets** Melting: **Fonte**

9. Supply the missing word

a. La **fonte** des glaces b. La **montée** du niveau de la mer c. Le rejet d'**eaux** usées
d. Les **déchets** industriels e. **L'augmentation** de la population f. Les **baleines** bleues
g. **Menacer** les espèces animales

10. Translate into French

a. **Sécheresses** b. **Rejet** c. **Déchets** d. **Menacer** e. **Réchauffement** f. **Augmentation** g. **Fonte**
h. **Eaux** i. **Embouteillages** j. **Niveau** k. **Mer** l. **Effet** m. **Serre** n. **Usines**

11. English to French translation

a. **L'utilisation de produits chimiques**
b. **L'élevage intensif**
c. **Le réchauffement climatique**
d. **La surconsommation de nourriture**
e. **Les déchets industriels**
f. **Le rejet d'eaux usées**
g. **Les embouteillages contribuent à la pollution de l'air**
h. **Les combustibles fossiles contribuent à l'effet de serre et au réchauffement climatique**
i. **La fonte des glaces cause la montée du niveau de la mer**
j. **Les baleines bleues et les ours polaires sont des animaux en danger**
k. **L'augmentation de la population mondiale contribue à l'épuisement des ressources naturelles**

Unit 4. Environment: global problems - Higher - Answers

1. Match up (section 1)

Floods – **Les inondations** *Greenhouse effect* – **L'effet de serre** *The rise* – **La montée**
Soils – **Les sols** *Melting of the ice caps* – **La fonte des glaces** *Warming* – **Le réchauffement**
Sea level – **Le niveau de la mer** *Animal species* – **Les espèces animales** *Extinction* – **La disparition**

2. Gapped phrases (sections 1 & 2) – Complete and translate

a. Le **gaspillage** de nourriture: ***Food waste*** b. L'**espèce** humaine: ***The human species***
c. Le **transport/trafic** aérien: ***Air transport/traffic***
d. La pollution de l'**air** et de l'**eau**: ***Air and water pollution*** e. Les gaz à effet de **serre**: ***Greenhouse gases***
f. La **montée** du niveau de la mer: ***Sea level rise***

3. Broken words (sections 2 & 3)

a. Les inonda**tions** b. Les ga**z** c. Le gaspi**llage** d. Les combusti**bles** e. Le niv**eau** f. La mon**tée**
g. La chas**se** h. Rout**ier** i. La dispa**rition** j. Aéri**en** k. La nourri**ture** l. La pén**urie**

4. Faulty translation – Correct the wrong translations (Sections 2 & 3)

a. *To **endanger*** b. ***Road** traffic* c. *To play a role* √ d. *To make visible* √ e. *To **stop***
f. ***Hunting*** g. *To **threaten***

5. Translate into English

a. ***Road traffic*** b. ***Hunting*** c. ***Fuels*** d. ***The rise*** e. ***The greenhouse effect*** f. ***Overconsumption***
g. ***Global warming*** h. ***The species*** i. ***World*** j. ***To stop*** k. ***The exhaustion*** l. ***To endanger***

6. Missing vowels

a. **L'espèce** b. **La chasse** c. **Épuisement** d. **Les combustibles** e. **Le trafic routier** f. **Le réchauffement**

7. Anagrams

a. **Espèces** b. **Niveau** c. **Chasse** d. **Épuisement** e. **Combustibles** f. **Fonte** g. **Glaces** h. **Réchauffement**

8. Sentence puzzle

a. La population mondiale n'arrête pas d'augmenter
b. L'effet de serre est augmenté par les activités humaines
c. L'espèce humaine impose de plus en plus sa présence dans le paysage
d. La fonte des glaces provoque des inondations en bord de mer
e. La disparition d'espèces animales menace la diversité de la faune
f. La température des océans continue de s'accroître

9. Complete the table

Hunting: **Chasse** ***Exhaustion***: Épuisement *Global warming*: **Réchauffement** *Fuels*: **Combustibles**
Waste: Gaspillage *Melting*: **Fonte** ***Floods***: Inondations *To increase*: **Augmenter**
Extinction: Disparition

10. Find in the wordsearch the French for the words listed in the box below

Hunting: **Chasse** *Fauna*: **Faune** *Diversity*: **Diversité** *Exhaustion*: **Épuisement** *Species*: **Espèce**
Flood: **Inondation** *Shortage*: **Pénurie** *Water*: **Eau** *Air*: **Air** *Melting*: **Fonte**

11. Guided translation

a. **La fonte des glaces** b. **La disparition d'espèces animales** c. **Les gaz à effet de serre**
d. **L'épuisement des ressources naturelles** e. **Le réchauffement climatique**
f. **La température des océans** g. **La population mondiale**

12. Translate into French

a. **La fonte des glaces** b. **Les activités de l'espèce humaine**
c. **La disparition d'espèces animales et végétales** d. **La montée du niveau de la mer**
e. **Le réchauffement climatique est un phénomène inquiétant**
f. **La pollution de l'air menace notre santé** g. **Les inondations sont de plus en plus fréquentes**
h. **Il y a beaucoup de gaspillage de ressources naturelles**
i. **Le trafic routier est responsable des émissions de gaz à effet de serre**
j. **L'utilisation de pesticides cause la pollution de l'eau**

UNIT 4 - Test - Answers (/100)

1. Vocabulary recognition: French-to-English translation (/15)

a. *The melting of the ice caps*	f. *To threaten*	k. *The landscape*
b. *The factories*	g. *The fires*	l. *The shortage*
c. *The greenhouse effect*	h. *The drought*	m. *The floods*
d. *Waste*	i. *The extinction*	n. *The fuels*
e. *Traffic jams*	j. *The sea*	o. *The overconsumption*

2. Syntax/Lexicogrammar – Split sentences (/5)

La population mondiale n'arrête	**pas d'augmenter**
La fonte des glaces provoque	**la montée du niveau de la mer**
L'effet de serre est accéléré	**par les activités humaines**
Le réchauffement climatique	**est accéléré par la pollution**
Il faut réduire le gaspillage	**des ressources**

3. Grammar/Morphology/Vocabulary – Tangled translation (/20)

a. Les **gaz** d'échappement des **voitures**

b. La **fonte** des **glaces**

c. La **disparition** des **espèces** animales

d. **Il y a** des **embouteillages**

e. L'**augmentation** de la population

f. **L'épuisement** des ressources naturelles

g. **Dans** les zones **côtières**

h. Le **gaspillage** de **nourriture**

i. Son **empreinte** sur l'**environnement**

j. La **montée** du **niveau** de la mer

k. Les **combustibles** fossiles

l. Le **réchauffement** climatique

4. Translate into French (/ 60 – each full sentence – 6 points)

a. **Les combustibles fossiles contribuent à l'effet de serre**

b. **La fonte des glaces cause la montée du niveau de la mer**

c. **Les baleines bleues et les ours polaires sont des espèces en danger**

d. **Les embouteillages sont une cause importante de la pollution de l'air**

e. **L'augmentation de la population est la cause principale de la pollution**

f. **La déforestation est une des causes du réchauffement climatique**

g. **La température des océans continue de s'accroître tous les jours**

h. **La montée du niveau de la mer cause des inondations en bord de mer**

i. **L'effet de serre (2) est accéléré par la pollution**

j. **La surconsommation joue un rôle important dans l'épuisement des ressources naturelles**

Unit 5. Environment: potential solutions

KEY VOCABULARY Foundation

1. Les solutions

Il faut... *It is necessary to...*
Nous devons... *We must...*
-acheter des produits durables *buy sustainable products*
-arrêter la déforestation *stop deforestation*
-bannir les pesticides: *ban pesticides*
-changer nos habitudes *change our habits*
-diminuer notre consommation *diminish our consumption*
-éviter les produits à usage unique *avoid single-use products*
-faire du covoiturage: *do carpooling*
-fermer les centres-villes aux voitures *close city centres to cars*
-interdire les engrais chimiques *forbid chemical fertilisers*
-limiter l'utilisation de l'eau *limit the use of water*
-planter des arbres: *plant trees*
-préserver les forêts: *preserve forests*
-recycler les déchets: *recycle rubbish*
-réduire les activités polluantes *reduce polluting activities*
-réduire le gaspillage: *reduce waste*
-réutiliser les objets: *reuse objects*
-utiliser les transports en commun *use public transports*
-utiliser un vélo pour les trajets courts *use a bike for short journeys*

2. Les problèmes (récapitulatif)

La disparition des espèces animales *The extinction of animal species*
La hausse des températures *The rise in temperatures*
La pollution de l'air/de l'eau/des sols *Air/water/soil pollution*
Le surpeuplement: *Overpopulation*
L'effet de serre: *The greenhouse effect*
L'épuisement des ressources *The exhaustion of resources*
Les emballages: *Packaging*
Les embouteillages: *Traffic jams*
Les gaz d'échappement des voitures *Car exhaust gases*
Les sécheresses: *Droughts*

1. Match up

Planter	***To forbid***
Bannir	***To plant***
Arrêter	***To preserve***
Réutiliser	***To ban***
Préserver	***To reduce***
Changer	***To buy***
Réduire	***To stop***
Acheter	***To reuse***
Éviter	***To avoid***
Interdire	***To close***
Fermer	***To change***

2. Broken words

a. Covoitu_ _ _ _ : *Carpooling*
b. Arb_ _ _ : *Trees*
c. Conso_ _ _ _ _ _ _ _ : *consumption*
d. For_ _ _ : *Forests*
e. Traj_ _ _ : *Journeys*
f. Eng_ _ _ _ : *Fertilisers*
g. Gaspi_ _ _ _ _ : *Waste*
h. Prod_ _ _ _ : *Products*
i. U_ _ _ _ _ _ _ _ : *To use*
j. Habi_ _ _ _ _ : *Habits*

3. Complete the English translations

a. Fermer les centres-villes: *To* __________ *the city centres*
b. Planter des arbres: *To plant* _________
c. Utiliser les transports en commun: *To use* _____________
d. Acheter des produits durables: *To* ___ *sustainable products*
e. Interdire les engrais chimiques: *To forbid chemical* ______
f. Changer nos habitudes: *To change our* _________
g. Limiter l'utilisation de l'eau: *To limit the use of* ________
h. Faire du covoiturage: *To do* ____________
i. Recycler les déchets: *To recycle* ____________
j. Réduire le gaspillage: *To reduce* ____________

4. Sentence puzzles

a. des Il réduire faut le ressources gaspillage
We must reduce the waste of resources
b. pesticides Nous bannir les devons
We must ban pesticides
c. arbres planter Il faut des
It is necessary to plant trees
d. les Nous recycler déchets devons
We must recycle rubbish
e. chimiques Il interdire faut engrais les
It is necessary to forbid chemical fertilisers
f. Nous utiliser un courts vélo les trajets devons pour
We must use a bike for short journeys
g. changer Il habitudes faut nos
It is necessary to change our habits

5. Choose the correct translation

a. Les combustibles: *fuels / droughts / gases*

b. La hausse: *reduction / vegetation / rise*

c. La surconsommation: *overcrowding / overconsumption / overuse*

d. Les embouteillages: *bottles / glass wasting / traffic jams*

e. Les emballages: *cigarette butts / gases / packaging*

f. La chasse: *hunting / fishing / waste*

g. La pollution des sols: *air pollution / noise pollution / soil pollution*

h. L'épuisement: *waste / exhaustion / rise*

i. La sécheresse: *waste / drought / fishing*

j. Le surpeuplement: *exhaustion / overpopulation / overconsumption*

6. Missing letters challenge

a. La cha_ _e

b. Les comb_stibles

c. La séchere_ _e

d. L_ surp_ _plement

e. Le_ e_bo_teillages

f. La hau_ _e

g. Le gasp_lla_e

h. Les ga_ d'écha_ _ement

i. Les habitu_es

j. Les en_rais chimi_ues

7. Break the flow

a. Ilfautfermerlescentres-villesauxvoitures

b. Nousdevonsplanterdesarbres

c. Ondoitpréserverlesforêts

d. Nousdevonsarrêterladéforestation

e. Ilfautfaireducovoiturage

f. Ondoitlimiterlutilisationdeleau

g. Ilfautdiminuernotreconsommation

8. Complete with the correct option

a. Il faut limiter le gaspillage des __________ naturelles

b. Nous devrions ________ les centres-villes aux voitures

c. On doit planter plus d'________

d. Il faut _________ du covoiturage autant que possible

e. Je devrais utiliser un vélo pour les trajets _________

f. Il faut utiliser les transports en ___________

g. On doit limiter la consommation de l'_________

h. Il faut recycler les _________

i. La chasse cause la disparition des _________ animales

j. Il faut changer nos _________ alimentaires

commun	**courts**	**espèces**	**faire**	**habitudes**
déchets	**ressources**	**arbres**	**eau**	**fermer**

9. Translate into French

a. Animal species

b. Public transport

c. The waste of resources

d. Chemical fertilisers

e. The rise in temperatures

f. The exhaustion

g. Rubbish

h. Trees

i. Hunting

10. Complete with a suitable word

a. Recycler les _____________

b. Réduire le ___________ des ressources

c. Réutiliser les __________

d. Changer nos ___________

e. Planter des ___________

f. Acheter des produits à usage _________

g. Utiliser un ________ pour les trajets courts

11. Translate into French

a. It is necessary to reduce the waste of natural resources

b. We must use public transport

c. We must ban the use of chemical fertilisers

d. It is necessary to plant more trees

e. It is better to use a bike for short journeys

f. We must recycle rubbish and reuse objects

g. We must limit our consumption of water

h. It is necessary to close city centres to cars

KEY VOCABULARY Higher

1. Les buts (the aims)

Pour combattre la pollution de l'air
To combat air pollution
Pour diminuer la déforestation
To diminish deforestation
Pour freiner la hausse des températures
To put the brakes on the rise of temperatures
Pour éviter les sécheresses
To avoid droughts
Pour limiter la surconsommation
To limit overconsumption
Pour lutter contre la pollution
To fight against pollution
Pour préserver la Terre
To preserve the Earth
Pour protéger les animaux
To protect animals
Pour protéger l'environnement
To protect the environment
Pour protéger les plantes: *To protect plants*
Pour ralentir l'épuisement des ressources
To slow down the exhaustion of resources
Pour réduire le gâchis de ressources
To reduce resources misuse
Pour sauver notre planète
To save our planet

2. Les solutions

Il faut... *It is necessary to...*
Nous devons... *We must...*
-bannir la chasse des espèces en voie de disparition
ban the hunting of endangered species
-bannir les pesticides: *ban pesticides*
-changer le comportement des individus
change people's behaviour
-diminuer les activités polluantes
diminish polluting activities
-diminuer notre consommation d'eau
diminish our water consumption
-éviter les produits à usage unique
avoid single-use products
-interdire la cueillette des espèces rares
forbid the picking of rare species
-limiter l'utilisation de l'eau potable
limit the use of drinkable water
-planter des arbres: *plant trees*
-recycler les déchets: *recycle rubbish*
-réutiliser les objets: *reuse objects*

1. Match up

Pour ralentir	***In order to reduce***
Pour protéger	***It is necessary to limit***
Pour préserver	***In order to save***
Pour réduire	***In order to avoid***
Pour sauver	***In order to fight against***
Pour éviter	***It is necessary to plant***
Pour lutter contre	***In order to preserve***
Il faut limiter	***It is necessary to ban***
Il faut bannir	***In order to slow down***
Il faut interdire	***In order to protect***
Il faut planter	***It is necessary to forbid***

2. Gapped translation

a. Pour protéger les animaux, il faut bannir la chasse des espèces en voie de disparition *In order to protect animals it is _____________ to ban the __________ of _______________ species*

b. Pour combattre la pollution de l'air, il faut diminuer les activités polluantes, comme utiliser la voiture

In order to ________ air pollution, it is necessary to _______ polluting activities, such as using the _____

c. Pour réduire le gaspillage des ressources et matériaux, nous devons recycler les déchets

In order to reduce the ____________ of resources and materials, we _______ recycle ___________

d. Pour protéger les plantes, il faut interdire la cueillette des espèces rares

In order to ___________ the plants, it is necessary to ___________ the picking of rare _________

3. Missing vowels

a. B_nn_r: *To ban*
b. Pl_nt_s: *Plants*
c. C_ _ _ll_tt_ : *Picking*
d. _rbr_s: *Trees*
e. R_l_nt_r: *To slow down*
f. Us_g_ : *Use*
g. Ch_ss_ : *Hunting*
h. _bj_ts: *Objects*
i. S_ _v_r: *To save*
j. L_tt_r: *To fight*

4. Broken words

a. Te____ : *Earth*
b. Rec____ : *To recycle*
c. Pla___ : *To plant*
d. Limi____ : *To limit*
e. Ar____ : *Trees*
f. Ob___ : *Objects*
g. Sau______ : *To save*
h. Cuei_____ : *Picking*
i. Pot_____ : *Drinkable*
j. Es______ : *Species*

5. Choose the correct translation

a. Les déchets: *objects / rubbish / trees*

b. La cueillette: *picking / landscape/ earth*

c. Les arbres: *trees / flowers / forests*

d. Potable: *rain / drinkable / disposable*

e. La pluie: *species / rain / weather*

f. La hausse: *rise / decline / waste*

6. Complete with the correct option from the box

a. _________ des arbres

b. La ________ des températures

c. Il ________ bannir

d. L'eau _________

e. Recycler les ________

f. Les __________ rares

espèces
hausse
déchets
faut
planter
potable

7. Anagrams

a. usHase: *Rise*

b. Arerbs: *Trees*

c. Rireédu: *To reduce*

d. erdIntire: *To forbid*

e. La Trree: *The earth*

f. etObjs: *Objects*

g. Freerin: *To brake*

h. rêFots: *Forests*

8. Sentence puzzle: find the correct order and translate into English

a. pesticides bannir les faut Il:

b. danger interdire en Nous animaux chasse devons la des:

c. arbres Nous planter des pouvons:

d. limiter Il faut de l'eau l'utilisation potable:

e. réutiliser Il objets faut les:

9. Complete the table

English	Français
The rise	
	Nous devons acheter
	Le gâchis
Single-use products	
	Le gaspillage
To plant trees	
	La surconsommation
It is necessary	
Soil pollution	

10. Find in the wordsearch the French for the words listed in the box below

A	R	B	R	E	S	P
I	A	O	U	P	O	R
Q	D	Z	S	T	S	O
S	U	T	A	G	R	D
F	R	B	G	Â	E	U
G	A	E	E	C	N	I
E	B	S	R	H	I	T
Y	L	S	L	I	E	S
O	E	A	P	S	R	W
C	Z	H	Q	T	F	E
D	É	C	H	E	T	S

Products:

Trees:

Use:

Sustainable:

Rubbish:

Misuse:

To brake:

Hunting:

11. Guided translation

a. L_ h________ : *The rise*

b. I_ f_________ : *It is necessary*

c. L'e___ p__________ : *Drinkable water*

d. L__ p___________ : *The products*

e. L_ g_______ : *The misuse*

f. L_ c________ : *Hunting*

g. L_______ c________ : *To fight against*

h. B________ : *To ban*

i. P____ r__________ : *In order to reduce*

j. L_ g____________ : *The waste*

k. L_ c______________ : *Behaviour*

12. Translate into French

a. In order to diminish deforestation

b. We must buy sustainable products

c. It is necessary to avoid single-use products

d. In order to limit overconsumption

e. Air and soil pollution

f. In order to reduce the misuse of resources

g. We must recycle rubbish and reuse objects

h. It is necessary to limit the use of drinkable water

i. We must collect rainwater for watering

j. It is important to preserve our forests

UNIT 5 - Test (/100)

1. Vocabulary recognition: French-to-English translation (/15)

a. Les produits durables

b. Les déchets

c. Les habitudes

d. La consommation

e. Fermer

f. Il faut

g. Polluante

h. Les engrais

i. Les arbres

j. Éviter

k. Le covoiturage

l. Nous devons

m. Bannir

n. Le gaspillage

o. Chimique

2. Syntax/Lexicogrammar – Split sentences (/5)

Il faut utiliser le vélo pour	faire du covoiturage
On doit éviter les produits à	de recycler les déchets
Nous devons	les trajets courts
Il est nécessaire	aux voitures
Il faut fermer les centres-villes	usage unique

3. Grammar/Morphology/Vocabulary – Tangled translation (/20)

a. Les **gases** d'échappement des **cars**

b. On **must** faire du **carpooling**

c. La **extinction** des **species** animales

d. Les produits à usage **single**

e. **To buy** des produits **sustainable**

f. Recycler les **waste industrial**

g. Changer nos **habits**

h. **To forbid** les **fertilisers** chimiques

i. **To ban** la **hunting**

j. L'**exhaustion** des ressources

k. **To diminish** notre **consumption**

l. **Reduce** les activités **polluting**

4. Translate into French (/ 60 – each full sentence – 6 points)

a. We must use a bike for short journeys

b. It is necessary to recycle rubbish and reuse objects

c. It is important to limit our consumption of water

d. We must reduce polluting activities such as air transport

e. It is important to avoid single-use products

f. We should ban the use of pesticides and chemical fertilisers

g. The exhaustion of resources is caused by overconsumption

h. The extinction of animal species is caused by deforestation

i. We must change our habits radically (*radicalement*) and consume less

j. To limit overconsumption, it is better to buy sustainable products

Unit 5. Environment: potential solutions - Foundation - Answers

1. Match up

Planter – ***To plant*** Bannir – ***To ban*** Arrêter – ***To stop*** Réutiliser – ***To reuse*** Préserver – ***To preserve*** Changer – ***To change*** Réduire – ***To reduce*** Acheter – ***To buy*** Éviter – ***To avoid*** Interdire – ***To forbid*** Fermer – ***To close***

2. Broken words

a. Covoitu**rage** b. Arb**res** c. Conso**mmation** d. For**êts** e. Traj**ets** f. Eng**rais** g. Gaspi**llage** h. Prod**uits** i. U**tiliser** j. Habi**tudes**

3. Complete the English translations

a. *To **close** the city centres* b. *To plant **trees*** c. *To use **public transport*** d. *To **buy** sustainable products* e. *To forbid chemical **fertilisers*** f. *To change our **habits*** g. *To limit the use of **water*** h. *To do **carpooling*** i. *To recycle **rubbish*** j. *To reduce **waste***

4. Sentence puzzles

a. **Il faut réduire le gaspillage des ressources** b. **Nous devons bannir les pesticides** c. **Il faut planter des arbres** d. **Nous devons recycler les déchets** e. **Il faut interdire les engrais chimiques** f. **Nous devons utiliser un vélo pour les trajets courts** g. **Il faut changer nos habitudes**

5. Choose the correct translation

a. Les combustibles: ***fuels*** b. La hausse: ***rise*** c. La surconsommation: ***overconsumption*** d. Les embouteillages: ***traffic jams*** e. Les emballages: ***packaging*** f. La chasse: ***hunting*** g. La pollution des sols: ***soil pollution*** h. L'épuisement: ***exhaustion*** i. La sécheresse: ***drought*** j. Le surpeuplement: ***overpopulation***

6. Missing letters challenge

a. La **chasse** b. Les **combustibles** c. La **sécheresse** d. **Le surpeuplement** e. **Les embouteillages** f. La **hausse** g. Le **gaspillage** h. Les **gaz d'échappement** i. Les **habitudes** j. Les **engrais chimiques**

7. Break the flow

a. Il faut fermer les centres-villes aux voitures b. Nous devons planter des arbres c. On doit préserver les forêts d. Nous devons arrêter la déforestation e. Il faut faire du covoiturage f. On doit limiter l'utilisation de l'eau g. Il faut diminuer notre consommation

8. Complete with the correct option

a. Il faut limiter le gaspillage des **ressources** naturelles b. Nous devrions **fermer** les centres-villes aux voitures c. On doit planter plus d'**arbres** d. Il faut **faire** du covoiturage autant que possible e. Je devrais utiliser un vélo pour les trajets **courts** f. Il faut utiliser les transports en **commun** g. On doit limiter la consommation de l'**eau** h. Il faut recycler les **déchets** i. La chasse cause la disparition des **espèces** animales j. Il faut changer nos **habitudes** alimentaires

9. Translate into French

a. **Les espèces animales** b. **Les transports en commun** c. **Le gaspillage des ressources** d. **Les engrais chimiques** e. **La hausse des températures** f. **L'épuisement** g. **Les déchets** h. **Arbres** i. **Chasse**

10. Complete with a suitable word

a. Recycler les **déchets** b. Réduire le **gaspillage** des ressources c. Réutiliser les **objets** d. Changer nos **habitudes** e. Planter des **arbres** f. Acheter des produits à usage **unique** g. Utiliser un **vélo** pour les trajets courts

11. Translate into French

a. Il faut réduire le gaspillage des ressources naturelles b. Nous devons utiliser les transports en commun c. Nous devons bannir les engrais chimiques d. Il faut planter plus d'arbres e. Il est mieux d'utiliser un vélo pour les trajets courts f. Nous devons recycler les déchets et réutiliser les objets g. Nous devons limiter notre consommation d'eau h. Il faut fermer les centres-villes aux voitures

Unit 5. Environment: potential solutions - Higher - Answers

1. Match up

Pour ralentir – ***In order to slow down*** Pour protéger – ***In order to protect***
Pour préserver – ***In order to preserve*** Pour réduire – ***In order to reduce***
Pour sauver – ***In order to save*** Pour éviter – ***In order to avoid***
Pour lutter contre – ***In order to fight against*** Il faut limiter – ***It is necessary to limit***
Il faut bannir – ***It is necessary to ban*** Il faut interdire – ***It is necessary to forbid***
Il faut planter – ***It is necessary to plant***

2. Gapped translation

a. *In order to protect animals it is* ***necessary*** *to ban the* ***hunting*** *of* ***endangered*** *species*
b. *In order to* ***combat*** *air pollution, it is necessary to* ***diminish*** *polluting activities, such as using the* ***car***
c. *In order to reduce the* ***waste*** *of resources and materials, we* ***must*** *recycle* ***rubbish***
d. *In order to* ***protect*** *the plants, it is necessary to* ***forbid*** *the picking of rare* ***species***

3. Missing vowels

a. **Bannir** b. **Plantes** c. **Cueillette** d. **Arbres** e. **Ralentir**
f. **Usage** g. **Chasse** h. **Objets** i. **Sauver** j. **Lutter**

4. Broken words

a. Te**rre** b. Recy**cler** c. Pla**nter** d. Limit**er** e. Ar**bres**
f. Obj**ets** g. Sau**ver** h. Cuei**llette** i. Pota**ble** j. Esp**èces**

5. Choose the correct translation

a. Les déchets: ***rubbish*** b. La cueillette: ***picking*** c. Les arbres: ***trees*** d. Potable: ***drinkable***
e. La pluie: ***rain*** f. La hausse: ***rise***

6. Complete with the correct option from the box

a. **Planter** des arbres b. La **hausse** des températures c. Il **faut** bannir d. L'eau **potable**
e. Recycler les **déchets** f. Les **espèces** rares

7. Anagrams

a. **Hausse** b. **Arbres** c. **Réduire** d. **Interdire** e. **La Terre** f. **Objets** g. **Freiner** h. **Forêts**

8. Sentence puzzle: find the correct order and translate into English

a. Il faut bannir les pesticides: ***It's necessary to ban pesticides***
b. Nous devons interdire la chasse des animaux en danger:
We must forbid the hunting of endangered animals
c. Nous pouvons planter des arbres: ***We can plant trees***
d. Il faut limiter l'utilisation de l'eau potable: ***It's necessary to limit the use of drinkable water***
e. Il faut réutiliser les objets: ***It's necessary to reuse objects***

9. Complete the table

The rise: **La hausse** ***We must buy***: Nous devons acheter ***The misuse***: Le gâchis
Single-use products: **Les produits à usage unique** ***Waste***: Le gaspillage
To plant trees: **Planter des arbres** ***Overconsumption***: La surconsommation
It is necessary: **Il faut** *Soil pollution*: **La pollution des sols**

10. Find in the wordsearch the French for the words listed in the box below

Products: **Produits** *Trees*: **Arbres** *Use*: **Usage** *Sustainable*: **Durable** *Rubbish*: **Déchets**
Misuse: **Gâchis** *To brake*: **Freiner** *Hunting*: **Chasse**

11. Guided translation

a. **La hausse** b. **Il faut** c. **L'eau potable** d. **Les produits** e. **Le gâchis** f. **La chasse**
g. **Lutter contre** h. **Bannir** i. **Pour réduire** j. **Le gaspillage** k. **Le comportement**

12. Translate into French

a. **Pour diminuer la déforestation** b. **Nous devons acheter des produits durables**
c. **Il faut éviter les produits à usage unique** d. **Pour limiter la surconsommation**
e. **La pollution de l'air et des sols** f. **Pour réduire le gâchis de ressources**
g. **Nous devons recycler les déchets et réutiliser les objets**
h. **Il faut limiter la consommation de l'eau potable**
i. **Nous devons récupérer l'eau de pluie pour l'arrosage** j. **Il est important de préserver nos forêts**

UNIT 5 - Test - Answers (/100)

1. Vocabulary recognition: French-to-English translation (/15)

a. **Sustainable products**

b. **Rubbish**

c. **Habits**

d. **Consumption**

e. **To close**

f. **It is necessary to**

g. **Polluting**

h. **Fertilisers**

i. **Trees**

j. **To avoid**

k. **Carpooling**

l. **We must/have to**

m. **To ban**

n. **Waste**

o. **Chemical**

2. Syntax/Lexicogrammar – Split sentences (/5)

Il faut utiliser le vélo pour	**les trajets courts**
On doit éviter les produits à	**usage unique**
Nous devons	**faire du covoiturage**
Il est nécessaire	**de recycler les déchets**
Il faut fermer les centres-villes	**aux voitures**

3. Grammar/Morphology/Vocabulary – Tangled translation (/20)

a. Les **gaz** d'échappement des **voitures**

b. On **doit** faire du **covoiturage**

c. La **disparition** des **espèces** animales

d. Les produits à usage **unique**

e. **Acheter** des produits **durables**

f. Recycler les **déchets industriels (1)**

g. Changer nos **habitudes**

h. **Interdire** les **engrais** chimiques

i. **Bannir** la **chasse**

j. L'**épuisement** des ressources

k. **Diminuer** notre **consommation**

l. **Réduire** les activités **polluantes**

4. Translate into French (/ 60 – each full sentence – 6 points)

a. **Nous devons utiliser un vélo pour les trajets courts**

b. **Il faut recycler les déchets et réutiliser les objets**

c. **Il est important de (2) limiter notre consommation d'eau**

d. **Nous devons réduire les activités polluantes comme/telles que le transport aérien**

e. **Il est important d' (2) éviter les produits à usage unique**

f. **Nous devrions bannir l'utilisation des pesticides et des engrais chimiques**

g. **L'épuisement des ressources est causé par la surconsommation**

h. **La disparition des espèces animales est causée par la déforestation**

i. **Nous devons changer nos habitudes radicalement et consommer moins**

j. **Pour limiter la surconsommation, il est mieux d' acheter des produits durables**

Unit 6. What I study, what I like/dislike and why

KEY VOCABULARY Foundation

1. Parler (talk) des matières scolaires
J'adore: *I love*
J'apprends: *I learn* / J'étudie: *I study*
Je déteste: *I hate*
Je préfère: *I prefer*
-les langues étrangères
foreign languages
-les matières scientifiques
scientific subjects

Ma matière préférée, c'est...
My favourite subject is...
-l'allemand: *German*
-l'anglais: *English*
-l'art dramatique: *drama*
-l'espagnol: *Spanish*
-l'histoire: *history*
-l'informatique: *IT*
-la chimie: *chemistry*
-le dessin: *art*

2. Dire ce que j'aime/je n'aime pas
Car c'est... *As it's...*
-difficile: *difficult*
-ennuyeux: *boring*
-enrichissant: *enriching*
-facile: *easy*
-fascinant: *fascinating*
-passionnant: *exciting*
-utile: *useful*
Car le/la prof est... *As the teacher is...*
-divertissant: *entertaining*
-intéressant: *interesting*
-motivant: *motivating*

Car le/la prof… *As the teacher...*
-a un bon/mauvais sens de l'humour
has a good/bad sense of humour
-est travailleur/sympa/marrant
is hard-working/nice/funny
-explique bien: *explains well*
-(ne) m'aide (pas) beaucoup:
(doesn't) help(s) me a lot
-ne se fâche jamais: *never gets angry*

3. Les verbes importants
Apprendre: *To learn*
Étudier: *To study*
Passer un examen: *To take an exam*

1. Match up

J'apprends	***I understand***
Les langues étrangères	***I learn***
Elle explique bien	***Subject***
Je comprends	***It's exciting***
C'est divertissant	***Foreign languages***
Je passe (un examen)	***I take***
Matière	***It's easy***
C'est passionnant	***She explains well***
J'étudie	***Useful***
C'est facile	***IT***
L'informatique	***It's entertaining***
Utile	***I study***

2. Complete the words

a. *Motivating*: Moti_ _ _ _
b. *Entertaining*: _ _ _ertissant
c. *Easy*: Fa_ _ _ _
d. *Chemistry*: La chi_ _ _
e. *History*: L'hist_ _ _ _
f. *A subject*: Une mat_ _ _ _
g. *He explains*: Il expl_ _ _ _
h. *To take (exam)*: Pas_ _ _
i. *Difficult*: Diffic_ _ _
j. *Fascinating*: Fascin_ _ _

3. Anagrams (section 2)

a. Uleti
b. tivMoant
c. yeuxnuEn
d. sionnPasant
e. mpaSy
f. rantMar
g. tissDiverant
h. ciFale
i. cileffiDi
j. téreInssant

4. Translate into English

a. C'est créatif
b. Le prof est sympa
c. C'est facile
d. J'adore le dessin
e. C'est ennuyeux
f. J'aime l'histoire
g. C'est utile
h. J'aime la chimie
i. Le prof m'aide
j. C'est divertissant
k. Il ne se fâche jamais
l. Elle est travailleuse

5. Spot and correct the wrong English translations

a. Divertissant: *Easy*
b. Motivant: *Motivating*
c. Ennuyeux: *Boring*
d. Passionnant: *Entertaining*
e. Marrant: *Hard-working*
f. Utile: *Enriching*
g. Sympa: *Mean*
h. Travailleur: *Lazy*
i. Inutile: *Useful*
j. Facile: *Easy*

6. Gapped translation

a. J'adore le français parce que c'est p____________ : *I love French because it is exciting*

b. J'_________ l'anglais depuis cinq ans: *I have been studying English for five years*

c. Ma ____________ préférée, c'est l'informatique car c'est _________ :
My favourite subject is ICT because it is useful

d. Au collège, j'___________ deux langues ____________ : *At school, I learn two foreign languages*

e. L'année prochaine, je vais _________ mes __________ de GCSE:
Next year, I am going to take my GCSE exams

f. Mon prof d'espagnol ____ un bon _________ de l'humour:
My Spanish teacher has a good sense of humour

g. Ma prof ____ sciences est très _______________ : *My science teacher is very hard-working*

h. _____ prof de maths ne se _______ jamais: *My maths teacher never gets angry*

7. Missing vowels

a. D_v_rt_ss_nt: *Entertaining*

b. P_ss_ _nn_nt: *Exciting*

c. _n_t_l_ : *Useless*

d. _t_l_ : *Useful*

e. M_t_v_nt: *Motivating*

f. S_mp_ : *Nice*

g. _nn_ _ _ _x: *Boring*

h. M_rr_nt: *Funny*

i. F_c_l_ : *Easy*

j. Tr_v_ _ll_ _r: *Hard-working*

8. Find in the wordsearch the French for the words listed in the box below

M	A	T	I	È	R	E	I	T
S	L	A	N	G	U	E	N	R
F	R	U	T	I	L	E	U	A
A	M	A	N	N	Y	U	T	V
C	O	D	P	U	N	L	I	A
I	T	C	R	T	V	X	L	I
L	I	B	R	I	G	S	E	L
E	V	M	A	L	K	V	X	L
X	A	J	M	E	A	R	Y	E
E	N	N	U	Y	E	U	X	U
Q	T	S	Y	M	P	A	L	R

Nice: S
Hard-working: T
Boring: E
Useless: I
Easy: F
Funny: M
Motivating: M
Subject: M
Language: L

9. Translate into French

a. It's creative

b. The teacher is nice

c. It's easy

d. I love art

e. It's boring

f. I like history

g. It's useful

h. I like chemistry

i. The teacher helps me

j. It's entertaining

k. He never gets angry

l. She is hard-working

10. Translate into French

a. I like drama because the teacher is funny and nice
b. I don't like maths because it's boring
c. At school, I learn two foreign languages: Spanish and German
d. My history teacher is very good. He explains things well
e. My English teacher helps me when I have a problem
f. My science teacher has a good sense of humour
g. My favourite subject is chemistry
h. I love French because it is exciting and useful

KEY VOCABULARY Higher

1. Ce que j'étudie (what I study)

J'apprends: *I learn* / J'étudie: *I study*
-l'art dramatique: *drama*
-la chimie: *chemistry*
-l'informatique: *IT*
-les langues étrangères: *foreign languages*

2. Dire quelles matières j'aime le plus (+)

Ce que j'aime étudier le plus, c'est les maths
What I like studying the most is maths
Mon cours préféré, c'est la biologie
My favourite lesson is biology
Selon moi, la meilleure matière c'est le dessin
According to me, the best subject is art

3. Dire quelles matières j'aime le moins (-)

Par contre/En revanche... *On the other hand...*
-ce que je ne supporte pas: *what I can't stand*
-ce que j'aime étudier le moins c'est...
what I like studying the least is...

4. Pourquoi j'aime/je n'aime pas mes sujets

J'adore cette matière parce que c'est...
I love this subject because it's...
Je déteste cette matière parce que c'est...
I hate this subject because it's...
-à mourir d'ennui: *boring to death*
-facile/dur: *easy/hard*
-fascinant/ennuyeux: *fascinating/boring*
-motivant/démotivant: *(de)motivating*
-utile/inutile: *useful/useless*

Je trouve cela facile/difficile
I find this easy/difficult
En plus, le/a prof est... *Moreover, the teacher is...*
-divertissant(e)/ennuyeux(euse)*entertaining/boring*
-patient(e)/impatient(e): *patient/impatient*
-sympathique/antipathique: *nice/unfriendly*
-travailleur(euse)/paresseux(euse)
hard-working/lazy
Il/Elle a un bon/mauvais sens de l'humour
He/She has a good/bad sense of humour

Et il/elle... *And he/she...*
-explique bien/mal les choses
explains things well/badly
-enseigne bien/mal: *teaches well/badly*
-m'aide/ne m'aide pas: *helps/doesn't help me*
-nous donne trop/peu de devoirs
gives us too much/little homework
-se fâche facilement/ne se fâche jamais
gets angry easily/never gets angry

Finalement, pendant les cours...
Finally, during the lessons...
-j'apprends beaucoup/je n'apprends rien
I learn a lot/I don't learn anything
-je comprends/je ne comprends pas
I understand/I don't understand

1. Match up (sections 1 to 3)

J'apprends	***It's art***
J'étudie	***What I have a horror of***
Ce que j'aime étudier	***On the other hand***
Mon cours préféré	***Foreign languages***
C'est la chimie	***I learn***
Par contre	***It's IT***
Ce dont j'ai horreur	***What I don't like***
C'est l'informatique	***My favourite lesson***
Les langues étrangères	***I study***
Ce que je n'aime pas	***It's chemistry***
C'est le dessin	***What I like studying***

2. Gapped translation (sections 2, 3 and 4)

a. Ce que j'aime étudier: *What I like* __________
b. Mon cours préféré: *My favourite* __________
c. La meilleure matière: *The* ________ *subject*
d. Ce que je ne supporte pas: *What I* _____________
e. Selon moi: ____________ *to me*
f. Je trouve cela difficile: *I* ________ *it difficult*
g. C'est à mourir d'ennui: *It is boring to* ________
h. Il a un bon sens de l'humour
He has a __________ *sense of humour*
i. Elle est divertissante: *She is* ________________

3. Translate into English – sections 2 to 4

a. Cette matière

b. C'est fascinant

c. Selon moi, c'est dur

d. Un bon sens de l'humour

e. C'est à mourir d'ennui

f. C'est divertissant

g. Elle est travailleuse

h. Je trouve cela facile

i. Je trouve cela dur

4. Broken words – section 4

a. Mat_____ : *Subject*
b. En pl___ : *Moreover*
c. Dev___ : *Homework*
d. D____ : *Hard*
e. Ut____ : *Useful*
f. Bi____ : *Well*
g. Ma___ : *Badly*

5. Missing vowels – Section 4

a. D_v_rt_ss_nt
b. F_c_l_
c. D_ff_c_l_
d. B_n
e. M_ _v_ _s
f. Tr_v_ _ll_ _r
g. P_r_ss_ _x

6. Choose the correct translation

a. J'apprends: *I learn / I study / I read*
b. Ennuyeux: *fun / exciting / boring*
c. Divertissant: *boring / rubbish / entertaining*
d. Informatique: *maths / art / IT*
e. Facile: *fun / hard / easy*
f. Dur: *hard / easy / fun*

7. Complete with the correct option from the box

a. J'apprends les ________ étrangères
b. Ce que j'aime le _______
c. Ma ___________ préférée
d. Je trouve _______ trop difficile
e. Je ne ______________ rien
f. J'_______ beaucoup dans les cours

comprends
matière
apprends
plus
langues
cela

8. Match the opposites

Ennuyeux	**Plus**
Facile	**Paresseux**
Bon	**Divertissant**
Bien	**Mauvais**
Moins	**Dur**
Patient	**Mal**
Travailleur	**Impatient**

9. Gapped English-to-French translation

a. La matière ____ j'aime le _______ : *The subject that I like the most*
b. Il a un ____ sens de l'_______ : *He has a good sense of humour*
c. Elle est ___________ et ________ : *She is hard-working and nice*
d. Il nous _______ trop de _______ : *He gives us too much homework*
e. Elle ___ m'________ pas: *She doesn't help me*
f. Il __________ bien les ________ : *He explains things well*
g. J'________ beaucoup dans les _______ : *I learn a lot in the lessons*

10. Complete the table

English	**Français**
I learn	
	Je comprends
I find	
He gives	
	Il ne se fâche pas
	Il enseigne
She explains	
	J'étudie
What I like	

11. Find in the wordsearch the French for the words listed in the box below

J'	É	T	U	D	I	E
A	J	I	E	J	L	M
P	E	L	U	E	D	W
P	T	E	Q	N'	O	R
R	R	N	I	A	N	F
E	O	S	L	I	N	N
N	U	E	P	M	E	K
D	V	I	X	E	T	E
S	E	G	E	P	A	U
Q	R	N	L	A	M	Z
C	T	E	I	S	P	O

I study:
He teaches:
He gives:
I find:
I learn:
I don't like:
He explains:
He teaches:

12. Guided translation

a. *He explains well*: I_ e________ b_______
b. *I find this hard*: J_ t_____ c___ d___
c. *I don't understand*: J__ n_ c_________ p____
d. *What I like*: C_ q___ j'_________
e. *I study science*: J'é_________ l_ s________
f. *He gives us*: I__ n______ d_________
g. *He gets angry easily*: I_ s_ f_____ f_________
h. *My favourite lesson*: M__ c____ p__________
i. *I don't learn anything*: J_ n'_________ r______
j. *I love IT*: J'a________ l'i_______________
k. *He teaches badly*: I__ e__________ m______

13. Translate into French

a. At school, I study maths, chemistry, two foreign languages, art, English, history and P.E.

b. The school subjects I like the most are English and Spanish

c. I like Spanish because the teacher is entertaining, the lessons are fun and I learn a lot

d. What I can't stand is maths because I find it difficult and the teacher explains things badly

e. My English teacher gives us too much homework and gets angry very easily

f. In the chemistry lessons, I don't understand much. On the other hand, in the maths lessons I learn a lot

UNIT 6 - Test (/100)

1. Vocabulary recognition: French-to-English translation (/15)

a. L'informatique

b. Une matière

c. J'apprends

d. Le dessin

e. Enrichissant

f. Facile

g. Parce que

h. Divertissant

i. Bon

j. Mauvais

k. Travailleur

l. Se fâcher

m. Passionnant

n. Étudier

o. L'allemand

2. Syntax/Lexicogrammar – Split sentences (/5)

Je pense que cette	l'allemand et le français
Par contre, ce que	c'est passionnant et motivant
Depuis un an, j'apprends	matière est très intéressante
Je trouve cela	à mourir d'ennui
La biologie,	je n'aime pas c'est l'histoire

3. Grammar/Morphology/Vocabulary – Tangled translation (/20)

a. **What** je préfere **to study**

b. C'est à mourir d'**boredom**

c. C'est **useless** dans la **life**

d. Ça **takes** du **time**

e. C'est **too complicated**

f. **According to** moi, c'est **relaxing**

g. Je **find** cela plutôt **easy**

h. J'adore **this subject** scolaire

i. Ce **of which** j'ai **horror**

j. Ce que je ne **stand** pas, c'est la **chemistry**

k. Je **myself interest** à cette matière

l. Mon **lesson** préféré, c'est le **art**

4. Translate into French (/ 60 – each full sentence – 6 points)

a. I like this school subject because it's exciting and motivating

b. Finally, what I hate is chemistry, because it's boring

c. I can't stand art, because I think it's useless in life

d. What I like to study the most is music

e. I don't like German, because it's too hard

f. On the other hand, maths is really useful

g. I like geography, but I don't like drama

h. What I truly hate is to take exams

i. I quite like Spanish because I find it easy and fun

j. My favourite lesson is English as it's very easy and creative

Unit 6. What I study, what I like/dislike and why - Foundation - Answers

1. Match up

J'apprends – ***I learn*** Les langues étrangères – ***Foreign languages*** Elle explique bien – ***She explains well***
Je comprends – ***I understand*** C'est divertissant – ***It's entertaining*** Je passe (un examen) – ***I take***
Matière – ***Subject*** C'est passionnant – ***It's exciting*** J'étudie – ***I study*** C'est facile – ***It's easy***
L'informatique – ***IT*** Utile – ***Useful***

2. Complete the words

a. Moti**vant** b. D**ivertissant** c. Fa**cile** d. La chi**mie** e. L'hist**oire**
f. Une mati**ère** g. Il expl**ique** h. Pass**er** i. Diffi**cile** j. Fascin**ant**

3. Anagrams (section 2)

a. **Utile** b. **Motivant** c. **Ennuyeux** d. **Passionnant** e. **Sympa**

f. **Marrant** g. **Divertissant** h. **Facile** i. **Difficile** j. **Intéressant**

4. Translate into English

a. **It's creative** b. **The teacher is nice** c. **It's easy** d. **I love art** e. **It's boring** f. **I like history**
g. **It's useful** h. **I like chemistry** i. **The teacher helps me** j. **It's entertaining** k. **He never gets angry**
l. **She is hard-working**

5. Spot and correct the wrong English translations

a. Divertissant: ***Entertaining*** b. Motivant: *Motivating* c. Ennuyeux: *Boring* d. Passionnant: ***Exciting***
e. Marrant: ***Funny*** f. Utile: ***Useful*** g. Sympa: ***Nice*** h. Travailleur: ***Hard-working*** i. Inutile: ***Useless***
j. Facile: *Easy*

6. Gapped translation

a. J'adore le français parce que c'est **passionnant**
b. **J'étudie** l'anglais depuis cinq ans
c. Ma **matière** préférée, c'est l'informatique car c'est **utile**
d. Au collège, j'**apprends** deux langues **étrangères**
e. L'année prochaine, je vais **passer** mes **examens** de GCSE
f. Mon prof d'espagnol **a** un bon **sens** de l'humour
g. Ma prof **de** sciences est très **travailleuse**
h. **Ma/Mon** prof de maths ne se **fâche** jamais

7. Missing vowels

a. **Divertissant** b. **Passionnant** c. **Inutile** d. **Utile** e. **Motivant**
f. **Sympa** g. **Ennuyeux** h. **Marrant** i. **Facile** j. **Travailleur**

8. Find in the wordsearch the French for the words listed in the box below

Nice: **Sympa** *Hard-working*: **Travailleur** *Boring*: **Ennuyeux** *Useless*: **Inutile** *Easy*: **Facile**
Funny: **Marrant** *Motivating*: **Motivant** *Subject*: **Matière** *Language*: **Langue**

9. Translate into French

a. **C'est créatif** b. **La/Le prof est sympa** c. **C'est facile** d. **J'adore le dessin** e. **C'est ennuyeux**
f. **J'aime l'histoire** g. **C'est utile** h. **J'aime la chimie** i. **Le prof m'aide** j. **C'est divertissant**
k. **Il ne se fâche jamais** l. **Elle est travailleuse**

10. Translate into French

a. J'aime l'art dramatique parce que le professeur est marrant et sympa
b. Je n'aime pas les maths parce que c'est ennuyeux
c. Au collège, j'apprends deux langues étrangères: espagnol et allemand
d. Mon professeur d'histoire est très bon. Il explique bien les choses
e. Mon professeur d'anglais m'aide quand j'ai un problème
f. Mon professeur de sciences a un bon sens de l'humour
g. Ma matière préférée, c'est la chimie
h. J'adore le français parce que c'est passionnant et utile

Unit 6. What I study, what I like/dislike and why - Higher - Answers

1. Match up (sections 1 to 3)

J'apprends – ***I learn*** J'étudie – ***I study*** Ce que j'aime étudier – ***What I like studying***
Mon cours préféré – ***My favourite lesson*** C'est la chimie – ***It's chemistry***
Par contre – ***On the other hand*** Ce dont j'ai horreur – ***What I have a horror of***
C'est l'informatique – ***It's IT*** Les langues étrangères – ***Foreign languages***
Ce que je n'aime pas – ***What I don't like*** C'est le dessin – ***It's art***

2. Gapped translation (sections 2, 3 and 4)

a. *What I like* ***studying*** b. *My favourite* ***lesson*** c. *The* ***best*** *subject* d. *What I* ***can't stand***
e. ***According*** *to me* f. *I* ***find*** *it difficult* g. *It is boring to* ***death*** h. *He has a* ***good*** *sense of humour*
i. *She is* ***entertaining***

3. Translate into English – sections 2 to 4

a. ***This subject*** b. ***It's fascinating*** c. ***According to me, it's hard*** d. ***A good sense of humour***
e. ***It's boring to death*** f. ***It's entertaining*** g. ***She is hard-working*** h. ***I find this easy*** i. ***I find this hard***

4. Broken words – Section 4

a. Mati**ère** b. En pl**us** c. Dev**oirs** d. D**ur** e. Ut**ile** f. Bi**en** g. Ma**l**

5. Missing vowels – section 4

a. **Divertissant** b. **Facile** c. **Difficile** d. **Bon** e. **Mauvais** f. **Travailleur** g. **Paresseux**

6. Choose the correct translation

a. J'apprends: ***I learn*** b. Ennuyeux: ***boring*** c. Divertissant: ***entertaining***
d. Informatique: ***IT*** e. Facile: ***easy*** f. Dur: ***hard***

7. Complete with the correct option from the box

a. J'apprends les **langues** étrangères b. Ce que j'aime le **plus** c. Ma **matière** préférée
d. Je trouve **cela** trop difficile e. Je ne **comprends** rien f. J'**apprends** beaucoup dans les cours

8. Match the opposites

Ennuyeux: **Divertissant** Facile: **Dur** Bon: **Mauvais** Bien: **Mal** Moins: **Plus**
Patient: **Impatient** Travailleur: **Paresseux**

9. Gapped English-to-French translation

a. La matière **que** j'aime le **plus** b. Il a un **bon** sens de l'**humour** c. Elle est **travailleuse** et **sympa**
d. Il nous **donne** trop de **devoirs** e. Elle **ne** m'**aide** pas f. Il **explique** bien les **choses**
g. J'**apprends** beaucoup dans les **cours**

10. Complete the table

I learn: **J'apprends** ***I understand***: Je comprends *I find*: **Je trouve** *He gives*: **Il donne**
He doesn't get angry: Il ne se fâche pas ***He teaches***: Il enseigne *She explains*: **Elle explique**
I study: J'étudie

11. Find in the wordsearch the French for the words listed in the box below

I study: **J'étudie** *He teaches*: **Il enseigne** *He gives*: **Il donne** *I find*: **Je trouve** *I learn*: **J'apprends**
I don't like: **Je n'aime pas** *He explains*: **Il explique** *He teaches*: **Il enseigne**

12. Guided translation

a. **Il explique bien** b. **Je trouve cela dur** c. **Je ne comprends pas** d. **Ce que j'aime**
e. **J'étudie les sciences** f. **Il nous donne** g. **Il se fâche facilement** h. **Mon cours préféré**
i. **Je n'apprends rien** j. **J'adore l'informatique** k. **Il enseigne mal**

13. Translate into French

a. **Au collège/À l'école, j'étudie les maths, la chimie, deux langues étrangères, le dessin, l'anglais, l'histoire et l'éducation physique**
b. **Les matières que j'aime le plus sont l'anglais et l'espagnol**
c. **J'aime l'espagnol car le professeur est divertissant, les cours sont marrants et j'apprends beaucoup**
d. **Ce que je ne supporte pas, ce sont les maths parce que je trouve cela difficile et le professeur explique mal les choses**
e. **Mon professeur d'anglais nous donne trop de devoirs et se fâche très facilement**
f. **Dans le cours de chimie, je ne comprends pas beaucoup. Par contre, dans le cours de maths j'apprends beaucoup**

UNIT 6 - Test - Answers (/100)

1. Vocabulary recognition - French-to-English translation (/15)

a. **IT**

b. **A subject**

c. **I learn**

d. **Art**

e. **Enriching**

f. **Easy**

g. **Because**

h. **Entertaining**

i. **Good**

j. **Bad**

k. **Hard-working**

l. **To get angry**

m. **Exciting**

n. **To study**

o. **German**

2. Syntax/Lexicogrammar – Split sentences (/5)

Je pense que cette	**matière est très intéressante**
Par contre, ce que	**je n'aime pas c'est l'histoire**
Depuis un an, j'apprends	**l'allemand et le français**
Je trouve cela	**à mourir d'ennui**
La biologie,	**c'est passionnant et motivant**

3. Grammar/Morphology/Vocabulary – Tangled translation (/20)

a. **Ce que** je préfere **étudier**

b. C'est à mourir d'**ennui**

c. C'est **inutile** dans la **vie**

d. Ça **prend** du **temps**

e. C'est **trop compliqué** **(1)**

f. **Selon** moi, c'est **relaxant**

g. Je **trouve** cela plutôt **facile**

h. J'adore **cette matière** **(1)** scolaire

i. Ce **dont** j'ai **horreur**

j. Ce que je ne **supporte** pas, c'est la **chimie**

k. Je **m'intéresse** à cette matière

l. Mon **cours** préféré, c'est le **dessin**

4. Translate into French (/ 60 – each full sentence – 6 points)

a. **J'aime cette matière scolaire parce que c'est passionnant et motivant**

b. **Finalement, ce que je déteste (2) c'est la chimie parce que c'est ennuyeux**

c. **Je ne supporte pas (2) le dessin, parce que je pense que c'est inutile dans la vie**

d. **Ce que j'aime étudier le plus, c'est la musique**

e. **Je n'aime pas l'allemand parce que c'est trop dur**

f. **Par contre, (2) les maths sont vraiment utiles**

g. **J'aime la géographie, mais je n'aime pas (2) l'art dramatique**

h. **Ce que je déteste (2) vraiment, c'est de passer des examens**

i. **J'aime assez l'espagnol, parce que je trouve cela facile et marrant**

j. **Mon cours préféré, c'est l'anglais car c'est très facile et créatif**

Unit 7. My post 16 plans

KEY VOCABULARY Foundation

1. Les options après le GCSE

Je vais... *I am going to...*

-aller au lycée: *go to sixth form*

-aller en première/terminale: *go to Year 12/13*

-chercher un travail: *look for a job*

-choisir la filière générale: *choose the academic pathway (A Levels/IB)*

-continuer mes études: *carry on my studies*

-étudier la physique/la chimie/le dessin *study physics/chemistry/art*

-faire un apprentissage: *do an apprenticeship*

-laisser tomber les maths: *drop maths*

-passer le baccalauréat: *take the baccalaureate*

-prendre une année sabbatique: *take a gap year*

-quitter l'école: *leave school*

-travailler comme coiffeur/vendeur/cuisinier *work as a hairdresser/sales assistant/chef*

2. Les adjectifs utiles

Parce que c'est... *Because it's...*

-créatif: *creative*

-dur: *hard*

-enrichissant: *enriching*

-facile: *easy*

-fascinant: *fascinating*

-passionnant: *exciting*

-utile: *useful*

3. Les expressions essentielles

L'année prochaine: *Next year*

Si c'est possible: *If it's possible*

Je pense que: *I think that*

Ensuite à l'université: *Afterwards at university*

Je veux: *I want*

Je voudrais: *I would like*

Je suis fort(e) dans cette matière: *I am good at this subject*

Cela me passionne: *I am passionate about this*

C'est important pour l'avenir: *It's important for the future*

Car ça m'intéresse: *As it interests me*

Car ça ne m'intéresse pas: *As it doesn't interest me*

1. Match (section 1)

Aller au lycée	***To do an apprenticeship***
Faire un apprentissage	***To go to Year 13***
Aller en terminale	***To go to sixth form***
Aller en première	***To go to Year 12***
Quitter l'école	***To look for a job***
Chercher un travail	***To continue my studies***
Étudier la chimie	***To study chemistry***
Laisser tomber	***To drop***
Travailler	***To leave school***
Continuer mes études	***To work***

2. Gapped translation (section 1)

a. Quitter l'école: *To* _________ *school*

b. Faire un apprentissage: *To do an* _____________

c. Travailler comme vendeur: *To work as a* _______

d. Étudier la chimie: *To* _________ *chemistry*

e. Aller au lycée: *To go to* _____________

f. Choisir la filière générale: *To* ___________ *the academic path*

g. Chercher un travail: *To look for a* ____________

3. Choose the correct translation (sections 1 & 2)

a. Laisser tomber: *to drop / to choose / to look for*

b. Passionnant: *easy / passionate / exciting*

c. Choisir: *to leave / to drop / to choose*

d. Utile: *useful / easy / challenging*

e. En terminale: *in Year 12 / in Year 13 / in Year 11*

f. En première: *in Year 12 / in Year 13 / in Year 11*

g. Vendeur: *chef / sales assistant / apprentice*

h. Chercher: *to drop / to look for / to learn*

4. Faulty translation (sections 2 & 3)

a. Je suis fort: *I am weak*

b. Cela me passionne: *I am emotional about this*

c. Ça ne m'intéresse pas: *This interests me a lot*

d. Si c'est possible: *If it is possible*

e. C'est dur: *It's easy*

f. Pour l'avenir: *For the future*

g. Ensuite: *Before*

5. Find in the wordsearch the French for the words listed in the box below

A	F	R	T	U	T	I	L	E
D	O	D	U	R	L	N	B	J
P	R	E	H	E	I	O	Z	E
R	T	L	B	H	S	A	V	P
E	O	A	C	C	G	U	B	E
M	S	N	A	R	A	R	T	N
I	C	I	D	E	V	E	R	S
È	B	M	C	H	E	I	A	E
R	N	R	U	C	N	D	V	Q
E	F	E	L	E	I	U	A	U
D	C	T	V	P	R	T	I	E
S	V	A	F	N	M	É	L	J

To look for
Job
Future
Hard
Useful
Year 12
Year 13
I think that
To study
Good at (strong)

6. Complete the table

English	**Français**
Job	
Hard	
	Année
	Je pense que
	Étudier
	Chercher
To work as	
Year 13	

7. Gapped English to French translation

a. ___ c'est possible: *If it is possible*
b. ________ un travail: *To look for a job*
c. Je _______ étudier: *I am going to study*
d. Car c'est ______ : *Because it's useful*
e. Laisser ________ : *To drop*
f. Une ______ sabbatique: *A gap year*
g. Je vais _______ : *I am going to leave*
h. Car c'est _____ : *As it's hard*
i. En _____________ : *In Year 13*
j. Je vais _______ : *I am going to do*
k. Continuer mes ________ : *To continue my studies*
l. _______ tomber: *To drop*
m. Chercher un ________ : *To look for a job*
n. Je ________ que: *I think that*
o. ___________ comme cuisinier: *To work as a chef*
p. En ____________ : *In Year 12*
q. La filière __________ : *The academic pathway*
r. _______ mon baccalauréat: *To take my baccalaureate*

8. Supply the missing words

a. Je vais c_ _ _ _ _ _ _ un travail
b. Je vais p_ _ _ _ _ mon baccalauréat
c. Je vais t_ _ _ _ _ _ _ _ _ comme cuisinier
d. Je vais a_ _ _ _ en terminale
e. S_ c'est possible, je vais faire un a_ _ _ _ _ _ _ _ _ _ _ _ _
f. Je vais q_ _ _ _ _ _ l'école
g. Je v_ _ _ travailler comme vendeuse
h. Je vais é_ _ _ _ _ _ les maths parce que c'est u_ _ _ _

9. Translate into French

a. I am going to go
b. I am going to look for
c. I am going to continue
d. I am going to choose
e. I am going to drop
f. I am going to do
g. I am going to work
h. I am going to take

10. English to French translation

a. If it is possible, I am going to continue my studies
b. I am going to take a gap year
c. I would like to do an apprenticeship
d. I am going to work as a chef in a restaurant
e. I am going to study maths because I am good at this subject
f. If it is possible, I am going to go to Year 12

KEY VOCABULARY Higher

1. Ce que je ferai après le collège

L'année prochaine... *Next year...*
Quand j'aurai fini mes études au collège...
When I finish my studies in middle school
J'aimerais beaucoup…
I would very much like to...
Je voudrais vraiment…
I would really want to...
-aller au lycée: *go to sixth form*
-aller en première: *go to Year 12*
-aller en terminale: *go to Year 13*
-passer le baccalauréat *take the baccalaureate*
Je prendrai une année sabbatique…
I will take a gap year...
-à l'étranger: *abroad*
-en Australie: *in Australia*
Je ferai un apprentissage pour devenir…
I will do an apprenticeship to become a...
-coiffeur/coiffeuse: *hairdresser*
-maçon: *builder*
-plombier: *plumber*
-vendeur/vendeuse: *sales assistant*
Je vais chercher un boulot dans…
I am going to look for a job in...
-l'hôtellerie: *hospitality*
-la restauration: *catering*
-la vente: *sales*

2. Si je continue mes études…

Je crois/pense que... *I believe/think that...*
Je vais choisir la filière générale/les A-Levels:
I am going to choose the academic pathway/A Levels
Je vais étudier… *I am going to study...*
Je vais laisser tomber… *I am going to drop...*
-le dessin: *art* / -l'art dramatique: *drama*

3. Ce que je vais faire à la faculté *(uni)*

Ensuite à l'université...
Afterwards at university...
Pour mes études supérieures...
For my further studies...
J'ai l'intention de faire une licence de droit:
I intend doing a law degree
J'envisage de faire un master de commerce
I contemplate doing a Masters of Commerce
Je ne sais pas encore ce que je veux faire
I don't know yet what I want to do
Je vais probablement étudier…
I am probably going to study...
-des langues étrangères: *foreign languages*
-des matières littéraires/scientifiques
literary/scientific subjects
Je n'ai aucune idée de ce que je vais étudier
I have no idea what I am going to study

1. Match up

Chercher	***To look for***
Lycée	***Year 12***
Maçon	***To drop***
Étudier	***Builder***
Chimie	***Year 13***
Première	***Sales assistant***
Vendeur	***Sixth form***
Choisir	***To choose***
Terminale	***Foreign***
Étrangères	***Chemistry***
Laisser tomber	***To study***

2. Gapped translation

a. Je vais faire: *I am going to* _________
b. Chercher un boulot: *To* _________ *a job*
c. Je vais étudier: *I am going to* _________
d. Un boulot dans la vente: *A job in* ____________
e. Quand j'aurai fini: *When I* ____________
f. Pour mes études supérieures: *For my* ___________
g. Je n'ai aucune idée: *I have* ___________
h. Je ne sais pas encore: *I don't* ___________ *yet*
i. Un master de commerce: *A* _______ *of Commerce*
j. Je veux faire: *I* __________ *to do*

3. Translate into English

a. Je vais laisser tomber la chimie

b. Je vais chercher un boulot comme vendeur

c. Je vais prendre une année sabbatique à l'étranger

d. Je vais étudier les langues étrangères

e. Je ferai un apprentissage

f. Je n'ai aucune idée de ce que je vais étudier

4. Broken words

a. Mat_____ : *Subject*
b. Étu_____ : *To study*
c. Ven___ : *Sales*
d. Cher___ : *To look for*
e. Bou___ : *Job*
f. Lan____ : *Languages*
g. Vra_____ : *Really*
h. Enc_____ : *Yet*

5. Missing vowels

a. J_ p_ns_ qu_
b. M_s _t_d_s
c. V_nd_ _r
d. Ch_rch_r
e. L'_nn_ _pr_ch_ _n_
f. B_ _l_t
g. _ppr_nt_ss_g_

6. Choose the correct translation

a. Chercher: *to learn / to study / to look for*

b. Encore: *already / later / yet*

c. Droit: *law / English / art*

d. Matières: *subjects / sectors / choices*

e. Vente: *job / hospitality / sales*

f. Dessin: *biology / chemistry / art*

7. Complete with the correct option from the box

a. Je vais étudier les _______ étrangères

b. Je vais aller en _______

d. Je n'ai ________ idée

e. Des __________ littéraires

f. Pour mes ________ supérieures

g. Je vais _______ avocat

matières
langues
études
aucune
devenir
terminale

8. Anagrams – Identify the hidden words

a. enVte

b. rmaleTein

c. emiPrère

d. Blotou

e. Chhererc

f. rentisAppsage

9. Sentence puzzle

a. licence J'ai de faire de droit l'intention une

b. baccalauréat Je passer mon voudrais

c. restauration Je vais chercher un dans la boulot

d. voudrais Je faire un apprentissage pour plombier devenir

e. aucune Je n'ai idée vais de ce que je étudier

f. dessin Je tomber vais laisser l'anglais et le

g. Je année prendrai une Australie sabbatique en

10. Complete the table

English	Français
I am going to look for	
	Un boulot
I am going to study	
I have no idea	
	Ce que je veux
	Laisser tomber
Foreign languages	
	Quand j'aurai fini
My studies	

11. Guided translation

a. *I have no idea*: J_ n'a_ a________ i________

b. *I am going to choose*: J_ v____ c_______

c. *What I want to study*: C_ q__ j_ v____ é_______

d. *Literary subjects*: L__ m_______ l___________

e. *Scientific subjects*: L__ m_______ s___________

f. *I am going to study*: J_ v_____ e____________

g. *I intend to*: J'a_ l'i__________ de

h. *I am going to drop*: J_ v___ l_______ t________

i. *I am going to look for a job in sales*: J_ v____ c_________ u_ b________ d____ l__ v__________

j. *I am going to take a gap year*: J_ v____ p________ u___ a________ s_____________

12. Translate into French

a. Next year, I am going to go to Year 12 because I would like to go to university

b. I am going to drop chemistry and maths because it's too difficult

c. I have no idea what I want to study after my GCSE exams

d. After my baccalaureate, I would like to go to university to do a degree in medicine

e. I don't know yet what I want to study, but I think I am going to continue studying foreign languages

f. I will do an apprenticeship to become a builder or a plumber

g. If I continue my further studies, I am probably going to study scientific subjects and maybe drama

UNIT 7 - Test (/100)

1. Vocabulary recognition: French-to-English translation (/15)

a. Un travail
b. Laisser tomber
c. En première
d. En terminale
e. L'école
f. Choisir
g. Je vais étudier
h. Utile
i. Je pense que
j. Si
k. Vendeur
l. Chercher
m. Passionnant
n. À l'étranger
o. Ensuite

2. Syntax/Lexicogrammar – Split sentences (/5)

Je suis fort	vendeur
Je vais aller	fascinant
J'adore cela car c'est	au lycée
Je voudrais travailler comme	année sabbatique
Je vais prendre une	dans cette matière

3. Grammar/Morphology/Vocabulary – Tangled translation (/20)

a. Je vais **take** mon baccalauréat
b. Je vais **drop** la chimie
c. Je vais **look for** un **job**
d. Je vais continuer mes **studies**
e. Je pense **that** je travaillerai **as** cuisinier
f. Ce **is not** une matière **useful**
g. **I will do** un **apprenticeship**
h. **Because** c'est **hard**
i. Je ne **know** pas **yet**
j. Je vais **go** en **Year 12**
k. C'est important pour l'**future**
l. Je **believe** que je vais **choose** le dessin

4. Translate into French (/ 60 – each full sentence – 6 points)

a. Next year, if it's possible, I am going to go to Year 12
b. Afterwards, I would like to study maths at university
c. I am going to study chemistry because I am good at this subject
d. I want to study languages because I am passionate about this
e. I think that after my exams, I will take a gap year
f. For my further studies, I intend to do a law degree
g. I will do an apprenticeship to become a builder or a plumber
h. For the moment, I am going to look for a job in catering
i. It's an important decision, therefore I prefer to take my time
j. After my exams, I am going to look for a job as a waiter

Unit 7. My post 16 plans - Foundation - Answers

1. Match (section 1)

Aller au lycée – ***To go to sixth form*** Faire un apprentissage – ***To do an apprenticeship***
Aller en terminale – ***To go to Year 13*** Aller en première – ***To go to Year 12***
Quitter l'école – ***To leave school*** Chercher un travail – ***To look for a job***
Étudier la chimie – ***To study chemistry*** Laisser tomber – ***To drop***
Travailler – ***To work*** Continuer mes études – ***To continue my studies***

2. Gapped translation (section 1)

a. *To* ***leave*** *school* b. *To do an* ***apprenticeship*** c. *To work as a* ***sales assistant*** d. *To* ***study*** *chemistry*
e. *To go to* ***sixth form*** f. *To* ***choose*** *the academic path* g. *To look for a* ***job***

3. Choose the correct translation (section 1 & 2)

a. Laisser tomber: ***to drop*** b. Passionnant: ***exciting*** c. Choisir: ***to choose*** d. Utile: ***useful***
e. En terminale: ***in Year 13*** f. En première: ***in Year 12*** g. Vendeur: ***sales assistant***
h. Chercher: ***to look for***

4. Faulty translation (sections 2 & 3)

a. Je suis fort: *I am* ***strong*** b. Cela me passionne: *I am* ***passionate*** *about this*
c. Ça ne m'intéresse pas: *This* ***doesn't interest*** *me ~~a lot~~* d. Si c'est possible: *If it is possible* √
e. C'est dur: *It's* ***hard*** f. Pour l'avenir: *For the future* √ g. Ensuite: ***Afterwards***

5. Find in the wordsearch the French for the words listed in the box below

To look for: **Chercher** *Job*: **Travail** *Future*: **Avenir** *Hard*: **Dur** *Useful*: **Utile** *Year 12*: **Première**
Year 13: **Terminale** *I think that*: **Je pense que** *To study*: **Étudier** *Good at (strong)*: **Fort**

6. Complete the table

Job: **Travail** *Hard*: **Dur** ***Year***: Année ***I think that***: Je pense que ***To study***: Étudier
To look for: Chercher *To work as*: **Travailler comme** *Year 13*: **Terminale**

7. Gapped English to French translation

a. **Si** c'est possible b. **Chercher** un travail c. Je **vais** étudier d. Car c'est **utile** e. Laisser **tomber**
f. Une **année** sabbatique g. Je vais **quitter** h. Car c'est **dur** i. En **terminale** j. Je vais **faire**
k. Continuer mes **études** l. **Laisser** tomber m. Chercher un **travail/emploi/boulot** n. Je **pense** que
o. **Travailler** comme cuisinier p. En **première** q. La filière **générale** r. **Passer** mon baccalauréat

8. Supply the missing words

a. Je vais **chercher** un travail b. Je vais **passer** mon baccalauréat c. Je vais **travailler** comme cuisinier
d. Je vais **aller** en terminale e. **Si** c'est possible, je vais faire un **apprentissage** f. Je vais **quitter** l'école
g. Je **vais** travailler comme vendeuse h. Je vais **étudier** les maths parce que c'est **utile**

9. Translate into French

a. **Je vais aller** b. **Je vais chercher** c. **Je vais continuer** d. **Je vais choisir** e. **Je vais laisser tomber**
f. **Je vais faire** g. **Je vais travailler** h. **Je vais prendre**

10. English to French translation

a. Si c'est possible, je vais continuer mes études
b. Je vais prendre une année sabbatique
c. Je voudrais faire un apprentissage
d. Je vais travailler comme cuisinier dans un restaurant
e. Je vais étudier les maths, parce que je suis fort(e) dans cette matière
f. Si c'est possible, je vais aller en première

Unit 7. My post 16 plans - Higher - Answers

1. Match up
Chercher – ***To look for*** Lycée – ***Sixth form*** Maçon – ***Builder*** Étudier – ***To study***
Chimie – ***Chemistry*** Première – ***Year 12*** Vendeur – ***Sales assistant*** Choisir – ***To choose***
Terminale – ***Year 13*** Étrangères – ***Foreign*** Laisser tomber – ***To drop***
2. Gapped translation
a. Je vais faire: *I am going to* ***do*** b. Chercher un boulot: *To* ***look for*** *a job*
c. Je vais étudier: *I am going to* ***study*** d. Un boulot dans la vente: *A job in* ***sales***
e. Quand j'aurai fini: *When I* ***finish*** f. Pour mes études supérieures: *For my* ***further studies***
g. Je n'ai aucune idée: *I have* ***no idea*** h. Je ne sais pas encore: *I don't* ***know*** *yet*
i. Un master de commerce: *A* ***Masters*** *of Commerce* j. Je veux faire: *I* ***want*** *to do*
3. Translate into English
a. ***I am going to drop chemistry*** b. ***I am going to looks for a job as a sales assistant***
c. ***I am going to take a gap year abroad*** d. ***I am going to study foreign languages***
e. ***I will do an apprenticeship*** f. ***I have no idea what I am going to study***
4. Broken words
a. Mati**ère** b. Étu**dier** c. Ven**te** d. Cher**cher** e. Bou**lot** f. Lan**gues** g. Vra**iment** h. Enc**ore**
5. Missing vowels
a. **Je pense que** b. **Mes études** c. **Vendeur** d. **Chercher**
e. **L'année prochaine** f. **Boulot** g. **Apprentissage**
6. Choose the correct translation
a. Chercher: ***to look for*** b. Encore: ***yet*** c. Droit: ***law*** d. Matières: ***subjects*** e. Vente: ***sales*** f. Dessin: ***art***
7. Complete with the correct option from the box
a. Je vais étudier les **langues** étrangères b. Je vais aller en **terminale** d. Je n'ai **aucune** idée
e. Des **matières** littéraires f. Pour mes **études** supérieures g. Je vais **devenir** avocat
8. Anagrams – identify the hidden words
a. **Vente** b. **Terminale** c. **Première** d. **Boulot** e. **Chercher** f. **Apprentissage**
9. Sentence puzzle
a. **J'ai l'intention de faire une licence de droit**
b. **Je voudrais passer mon baccalauréat**
c. **Je vais chercher un boulot dans la restauration**
d. **Je voudrais faire un apprentissage pour devenir plombier**
e. **Je n'ai aucune idée de ce que je vais étudier**
f. **Je vais laisser tomber l'anglais et le dessin** (subjects can be swapped here)
g. **Je prendrai une année sabbatique en Australie**
10. Complete the table
I am going to look for: **Je vais chercher** ***A job***: Un boulot *I am going to study*: **Je vais étudier**
I have no idea: **Je n'ai aucune idée** ***What I want***: Ce que je veux ***To drop***: Laisser tomber
Foreign languages: **Les langues étrangères** ***When I finish***: Quand j'aurai fini *My studies*: **Mes études**
11. Guided translation
a. **Je n'ai aucune idée** b. **Je vais choisir** c. **Ce que je veux étudier** d. **Les matières littéraires**
e. **Les matières scientifiques** f. **Je vais étudier** g. **J'ai l'intention de** h. **Je vais laisser tomber**
i. **Je vais chercher un boulot dans la vente** j. **Je vais prendre une année sabbatique**
12. Translate into French
a. **L'année prochaine, je vais aller en première parce que je voudrais aller à l'université**
b. **Je vais laisser tomber la chimie et les maths parce que c'est trop difficile**
c. **Je n'ai aucune idée de ce que je vais étudier après mes examens de GCSE**
d. **Après mon baccalauréat, je voudrais aller à l'université pour faire une licence de médecine**
e. **Je ne sais pas encore ce que je veux étudier, mais je pense que je vais continuer à étudier les langues étrangères**
f. **Je ferai un apprentissage pour devenir maçon ou plombier**
g. **Si je continue mes études supérieures, je vais probablement étudier des matières scientifiques et peut-être l'art dramatique**

UNIT 7 - Test - Answers (/100)

1. Vocabulary recognition: French-to-English translation (/15)

a. **A job**

b. **To drop**

c. **In Year 12**

d. **In Year 13**

e. **School**

f. **To choose**

g. **I am going to study**

h. **Useful**

i. **I think that**

j. **If**

k. **Sales assistant**

l. **To look for**

m. **Exciting**

n. **Abroad**

o. **Afterwards/Then**

2. Syntax/Lexicogrammar – Split sentences (/5)

Je suis fort	**dans cette matière**
Je vais aller	**au lycée**
J'adore cela car c'est	**fascinant**
Je voudrais travailler comme	**vendeur**
Je vais prendre une	**année sabbatique**

3. Grammar/Morphology/Vocabulary – Tangled translation (/20)

a. Je vais **passer** mon baccalauréat

b. Je vais **laisser tomber (1)** la chimie

c. Je vais **chercher** un **travail/boulot/emploi**

d. Je vais continuer mes **études**

e. Je pense **que** je travaillerai **comme** cuisinier

f. Ce **n'est pas (1)** une matière **utile**

g. **Je ferai** un **apprentissage**

h. **Parce que (1)** c'est **dur**

i. Je ne **sais** pas **encore**

j. Je vais **aller** en **première**

k. C'est important pour l'**avenir**

l. Je **crois** que je vais **choisir** le dessin

4. Translate into French (/ 60 – each full sentence – 6 points)

a. **L'année prochaine, si c'est possible (2), je vais aller en première**

b. **Ensuite, je voudrais étudier les maths à l' université**

c. **Je vais étudier la chimie parce que je suis bon(ne) dans cette matière**

d. **Je veux étudier les langues parce que cela me passionne (2)**

e. **Je pense qu' après mes examens, je prendrai une année sabbatique**

f. **Pour mes études supérieures, j'ai l'intention de faire une licence de droit**

g. **Je ferai un apprentissage pour devenir maçon ou plombier**

h. **Pour le moment, je vais chercher un travail/boulot/emploi dans la restauration**

i. **C'est une décision importante, donc je préfère prendre mon temps**

j. **Après mes examens, je vais chercher un boulot comme serveur**

Unit 8. What job I would like to do and why

KEY VOCABULARY Foundation

1. Les métiers *(jobs)*

Après mes études... *After my studies...*
Je voudrais devenir/travailler comme
I would like to become/work as a/an
Je serai... *I will be a/an...*
-artisan: *craftsman*
-avocat(e): *lawyer*
-chirurgien(ne): *surgeon*
-coiffeur(euse): *hairdresser*
-cuisinier(ère): *chef*
-docteur: *doctor*
-électricien(ne): *electrician*
-enseignant(e): *teacher*
-infirmier(ère): *nurse*
-informaticien(ne): *IT worker*
-ingénieur(e): *engineer*
-musicien(ne): *musician*
-plombier: *plumber*
-professeur(e): *teacher*
-vendeur(euse): *shop assistant*
-vétérinaire: *vet*

2. Le type de métier que je voudrais

Je voudrais un emploi...
I would like a/an... job
-de bureau: *office*
-en plein air: *outdoor*
in the... sector
-dans le bénévolat: *volunteering*
-dans l'industrie: *industry*
-dans le commerce: *retail*
-dans l'informatique: *IT*

3. Pourquoi je voudrais ce métier

Parce que c'est... *Because it is...*
-agréable: *pleasant*
-bien payé: *well-paid*
-gratifiant: *rewarding*
-important: *important*
-utile: *useful*
-varié: *varied*
Et parce que cela permet…
And it allows you to...
-d'aider les autres: *help others*
-de gagner beaucoup d'argent
to earn a lot of money
-de travailler en contact avec la nature
to work in touch with nature
-de voyager: *travel*

1. Complete the table (section 1)

English	Français (masculine)	Français (feminine)
electrician	électricien	
	infirmier	
lawyer	avocat	
		coiffeuse
surgeon		
	vendeur	
	cuisinier	
		informaticienne
musician		

2. Broken words (section 1)

a. Cuisi_ _ _ _ _ : *Chef* (F)
b. Plom_ _ _ _ : *Plumber* (M)
c. Ingé_ _ _ _ _ : *Engineer* (M)
d. Em_ _ _ _ : *Job*
e. Musi_ _ _ _ _ _ : *Musician* (F)
f. Trava_ _ _ _ _ : *To work*
g. Avo_ _ _ _ : *Lawyer* (F)
h. Étu_ _ _ : *Studies*

3. Translate into English (section 1)

a. Enseignant:
b. Vendeur:
c. Devenir:
d. Je serai:
e. Artisan:
f. Chirurgien:
g. Cuisinier:

4. Faulty translation (sections 1 & 2) – Correct the wrong English translations

a. Je voudrais un bon emploi: *I would like a good salary*
b. Un emploi de bureau: *An outdoor job*
c. Un emploi dans le bénévolat: *A job in the army*
d. Je voudrais travailler: *I would like to travel*
e. Je serai coiffeuse: *I will be a builder*
f. Je voudrais devenir: *I would like to travel*
g. Un emploi en plein air: *An outdoor job*
h. Un emploi dans l'informatique: *An IT job*

5. Circle the six positive adjectives on the list below and translate them into English (section 2)

a. Agréable	e. Bien payé	i. Gratifiant
b. Mal payé	f. Utile	j. Honteux
c. Fatigant	g. Important	k. Sale
d. Dur	h. Fascinant	i. Mauvais

6. Complete the English translation

a. Je voudrais un emploi dans le bénévolat: *I would like a job in the* ________________ *sector*

b. Après mes études, je serai ingénieur: *After my* ________, *I will be an* ______________

c. Un jour, je voudrais devenir chirurgien: *One* _______, *I would like to become a* ___________

d. Je serai pilote, car cela permet de voyager: *I will be a* _______, *because it allows you to* _______

e. Je voudrais un emploi en plein air: *I would like an* __________ _____

f. J'aimerais un boulot dans le commerce: *I would like a job in the* _________ *sector*

g. Je voudrais devenir coiffeuse comme ma mère: *I would like to become a* __________ *like my mother*

h. Je serai bénévole, car cela permet d'aider les autres:
I will be a ___________ *because it allows you to* _________ *others*

7. Find in the wordsearch the French for the words listed in the box below (sections 1 & 2)

D	O	C	T	E	U	R	I	A
R	E	I	M	R	I	F	N	I
S	N	T	B	L	E	S	G	F
R	S	U	É	C	N	Q	É	J
T	E	S	N	X	P	E	N	E
F	I	N	É	Z	L	D	I	S
U	G	P	V	A	E	J	E	U
J	N	E	O	E	I	K	U	E
I	A	I	L	P	N	O	R	D
E	N	L	A	B	A	L	M	N
R	T	A	T	F	I	M	N	E
S	J	E	S	E	R	A	I	V

Nurse: I

Doctor: D

Teacher: E

Outdoor: E

Engineer: I

Sales assistant: V

Volunteering: B

I will be: J

8. Complete (section 3)

a. Gagner beaucoup d'a_ _ _ _ _

b. Un emploi b_ _ _ payé

c. Je s_ _ _ _ enseignante

d. Parce q_ _ c'est varié

e. Un emploi d_ _ _ l'industrie

f. Un emploi g_ _ _ _ _ _ _ _ _

g. Cela p_ _ _ _ _ de voyager

h. Aider les a_ _ _ _ _

i. En contact a_ _ _ la nature

j. Je serai v_ _ _ _ _ _

9. Translate into French

a. Job:

b. Lawyer (F):

c. Money:

d. Varied

e. Well-paid:

f. Sales assistant:

g. Pleasant:

h. I will be:

10. Guided translation

a. *A job in the industry sector*: U__ e________ d____ l'___________

b. *I would like to become*: J__ v__________ d___________

c. *An outdoor job*: U__ e________ e__ p_______ a_____

d. *I will be a teacher*: J__ s_______ e____________

e. *Because it is pleasant*: C___ c'e____ a____________

f. *I would like to work as*: J__ v_______ t__________ c_________

g. *I would like an office job*: J__ v______ u___ e_______ d_ b______

h. *A job in the volunteering sector*: U_ e_____ d____ l_ b__________

11. English-to-French translation

a. I would like to work as a pilot because this allows you to travel

b. I would like to work as a teacher because it is rewarding

c. I will be a surgeon because it is a well-paid job

d. I would like to become a lawyer because it is important

e. I would like an outdoor job in agriculture

f. I would like to work as a taxi driver because it's varied

KEY VOCABULARY Higher

1. Ce que je veux faire après mes études

Après mes études... *After my studies...*
Une fois que j'ai mon diplôme...
Once I have my diploma...
J'aimerais travailler comme…
I would like to work as...
Je voudrais devenir… *I would like to become...*
-chirurgien(ne): *surgeon*
-enseignant(e): *teacher*
-informaticien(ne): *IT worker*
-vendeur(euse): *shop assistant*

2. Pourquoi je veux choisir cette profession

Je rêve de cette carrière car c'est...
I dream of this career as it's...
Je (ne) veux (pas) faire ce travail parce que cela semble…
I (don't) want to do this work because it seems...
-exigeant: *demanding* / -fatigant: *tiring*
-gratifiant: *rewarding* / -lucratif: *lucrative*
-stressant: *stressful*
À mon avis/Selon moi...
In my opinion/According to me...
C'est une activité qui est lucrative
It's an activity which is lucrative
C'est un secteur qui est en plein essor
It's a sector which is fast-growing
C'est une industrie qui est très tendance
It's an industry which is very trendy
Cette profession me permettra…
This profession will allow me...
-d'aider les autres: *to help others*
-de travailler en équipe: *to work as a team*
-de voyager: *to travel*

3. Les conseils *(advice)* de mes proches

Selon mes amis... *According to my friends...*
Mes parents me disent... *My parents tell me...*
Mon frère me dit que... *My brother tells me that...*
Mes professeurs pensent que...
My teachers think that...
-je devrais faire carrière dans la vente
I should make a career in sales
-je devrais faire médecine à la faculté
I should do medecine at university
-je devrais travailler comme… *I should work as a/an*
-architecte: *architect*
-instructeur de sport: *sport instructor*
-journaliste: *journalist*

4. Mon avis *(My opinion)*

Quant à moi, je préfère… *As for me, I prefer...*
-les boulots de bureau: *office jobs*
-les emplois en plein air: *outdoor jobs*
-le travail indépendant: *independent work*
-les travaux manuels: *manual work*

1. Match up

La vente	***Others***
Fatigant	***Fast-growing***
En plein essor	***Once***
Artisan	***Sales***
Voyager	***Tiring***
Autres	***Sales assistant***
Vendeur	***To travel***
Une fois	***As***
Comme	***Craftsman***

2. Gapped translation

a. Après mes études: *After my* _________
b. À mon avis: *In my* _________
c. Selon mes amis: _________ *my friends*
d. Mes parents me disent: *My parents*______ *me*
e. Je devrais faire: *I* _________ *do*
f. Je voudrais devenir: *I should* _________
g. C'est très tendance: *It's very* _________

3. Broken words

a. Les au_ _ _ _: *The others*
b. Équi_ _: *Team*
c. Cette car_ _ _ _ _: *This career*
d. Une indus_ _ _ _: *An industry*
e. Choi_ _ _: *To choose*
f. La ven_ _: *Sales*

4. Faulty translation – Correct the wrong English translations

a. Les emplois de bureau: *Outdoor jobs*
b. Quant à moi: *According to me*
c. Les travaux manuels: *Manual work*
d. Je devrais travailler: *I should go*
e. Mon frère me dit que: *My brother thinks that*
f. Mes profs pensent que: *My teachers say that*
g. Un secteur en plein essor: *A fast-growing*

5. Translate into English (All sections)

a. Un emploi indépendant
b. Un emploi de bureau
c. Quant à moi
d. En plein essor
e. Fatigant
f. En plein air
g. Mes amis me disent que
h. Je devrais faire médecine
i. Mes professeurs pensent que
j. Cela semble exigeant
k. Travailler en équipe
l. Une carrière dans la vente

6. Missing vowels (jobs)

a. _v_c_t
b. _rt_s_n
c. c_mpt_bl_
d. _ns_ _gn_nt
e. _nf_rm_t_c_ _n
f. _rch_t_ct_

7. Complete with the missing words

a. Un ________ indépendant
b. En _______ essor
c. Cela _________ exigeant
d. Je ________ devenir artisan
e. Une carrière ______ la vente
f. Après _____ études

8. Sentence puzzle

a. secteur c'est un et en essor L'informatique, fascinant plein
b. devenir à moi, je pense je Quant que avocat devrais
c. comptable études, Après mes je travailler comme voudrais
d. carrière Mes disent que je amis vente devrais faire dans la
e. boulots à moi, je les de bureau Quant préfère
f. Mon que comme frère me dit je travailler journaliste devrais

9. Complete the table

English	**Français**
	En plein essor
I would like to become	
	Les boulots de bureau
According to me	
	Quant à moi
	Mon frère me dit que
Demanding	
	Faire carrière
A manual job	

10. Find in the wordsearch the French for the words listed in the box below

F	A	T	I	G	A	N	T
Y	U	A	N	T	B	D	S
B	T	R	D	P	O	A	G
U	R	T	U	L	U	H	V
R	E	I	S	O	L	C	E
E	S	S	T	U	O	Z	N
A	R	A	R	E	T	R	T
U	D	N	I	V	M	X	E
A	V	O	E	C	N	Q	E
C	A	R	R	I	È	R	E
L	R	U	E	T	C	E	S

Tiring
Others
Sales
Sector
Craftsman
Job
Industry
Office
Career

11. Guided translation

a. *Fast-growing*: E_ p____ e_______
b. *According to me*: S_______ m____
c. *I would like to become*: J_ v_______ d_______
d. *An office job*: U_ e_______ d_ b_________
e. *I would like to work*: J_ v_______ t________
f. *After my studies*: A______ m___ é_________
g. *In sales*: D_____ l_ v__________
h. *It will allow me*: C____ m___ p___________
i. *Sports instructor*: I_________ d_ s________

12. Translate into French

a. After my studies, I would like to work as a surgeon
b. I like this job, as it will allow me to travel
c. It seems demanding, but not stressful
d. I should make a career in sales
e. My parents tell me that I should study medicine
f. My brother tells me I should work as a teacher
g. I prefer outdoor jobs, so I would like to be a farmer
h. This job will allow me to help others
i. I dream of this career, as I think this profession is fascinating

UNIT 8 - Test (/100)

1. Vocabulary recognition: French-to-English translation (/15)

a. Mes études
b. Devenir
c. Plombier
d. Je voudrais
e. Un emploi
f. Fatigant
g. Je serai
h. Artisan
i. Bureau
j. En plein air
k. Aider
l. Vendeur
m. Passionnant
n. Cela permet de
o. Bien payé

2. Syntax/Lexicogrammar – Split sentences (/5)

Cela permet	secteur qui est assez lucratif
Je veux travailler	de voyager
Je voudrais un emploi	dans le bénévolat
À mon avis, c'est un	plein air
Je voudrais un boulot en	en contact avec la nature

3. Grammar/Morphology/Vocabulary – Tangled translation (/20)

a. Je **will be** plombier
b. Je **would like** un boulot **well-paid**
c. **According to** mes **friends**
d. Je **want** faire **this job**
e. Je voudrais avoir un boulot **outdoors**
f. Je voudrais **become** ingénieur
g. **I prefer** le travail **independent**
h. C'est une **industry which is** lucrative
i. Je voudrais **work** comme **craftsman**
j. Mes parents me **tell that** je devrais être médecin
k. C'est très **trendy** en **this** moment
l. Je voudrais faire **career** dans la **sales**

4. Translate into French (/ 60 – each full sentence – 6 points)

a. Once I am a graduate, I would like to become an accountant
b. I like this profession because it will allow me to travel
c. My parents tell me that I should study medicine at university
d. I prefer independent work, so I would like to be a craftsman
e. My friends tell me that I should work as a sports instructor
f. As for me, I prefer outdoor jobs, so I could be a farmer
g. In my opinion, it's a sector which is fast-growing at the moment
h. According to me, it's an industry which is quite lucrative today
i. My brother tells me I should make a career in retail
j. After my studies, I would like to work as a surgeon because it's a well-paid job

Unit 8. What job I would like to do and why - Foundation - Answers

1. Complete the table (section 1)

English	Français (masculine)	Français (feminine)
electrician	électricien	**électricienne**
nurse	infirmier	**infirmière**
lawyer	avocat	**avocate**
hairdresser	**coiffeur**	coiffeuse
surgeon	**chirurgien**	**chirurgienne**
sales assistant	vendeur	**vendeuse**
chef	cuisinier	**cuisinière**
IT worker	informaticien	informaticienne
musician	**musicien**	**musicienne**

2. Broken words (section 1)
a. Cuisi**nière** b. Plom**bier** c. Ingé**nieur** d. Em**ploi** e. Musi**cienne** f.Trava**iller** g. Avo**cate** h. Étu**des**
3. Translate into English (section 1)
a. ***Teacher*** b. ***Sales assistant*** c. ***To become*** d. ***I will be*** e. ***Craftsman*** f. ***Surgeon*** g. ***Chef***
4. Faulty translation (sections 1 & 2) – Correct the wrong English translations
a. *I would like a good* ***job*** b. *An* ***office*** *job* c. *A job in the* ***volunteering sector*** d. *I would like to* ***work***
e. *I will be a* ***hairdresser*** f. *I would like to* ***become*** g. *An outdoor job* √ h. *An IT job* √
5. Circle the six positive adjectives on the list below and translate them into English (Section 2)
a. **Agréable: *Pleasant*** e. **Bien payé: *Well-paid*** i. **Gratifiant: *Rewarding***
b. Mal payé f. **Utile: *Useful*** j. Honteux
c. Fatigant g. **Important: *Important*** k. Sale
d. Dur h. **Fascinant: *Fascinating*** i. Mauvais
6. Complete the English translation
a. *I would like a job in the* ***volunteering*** *sector* b. *After my* ***studies,*** *I will be an* ***engineer***
c. *One* ***day****, I would like to become a* ***surgeon*** d. *I will be a* ***pilot****, because it allows you to* ***travel***
e. *I would like an* ***outdoor job*** f. *I would like a job in the* ***retail*** *sector*
g. *I would like to become a* ***hairdresser*** *like my mother*
h. *I will be a* ***volunteer*** *because it allows you to* ***help*** *others*
7. Find in the wordsearch the French for the words listed in the box below (Sections 1 and 2)
Nurse: **Infirmier** *Doctor*: **Docteur** *Teacher*: **Enseignant** *Outdoor*: **En plein air** *Engineer*: **Ingénieur**
Sales assistant: **Vendeuse** *Volunteering*: **Bénévolat** *I will be*: **Je serai**
8. Complete (section 3)
a. Gagner beaucoup d'**argent** b. Un emploi **bien** payé c. Je **serai** enseignante d. Parce q**ue** c'est varié
e. Un emploi **dans** l'industrie f. Un emploi **gratifiant** g. Cela **permet** de voyager h. Aider les a**utres**
i. En contact **avec** la nature j. Je serai v**endeur**
9. Translate into French
a. *Job*: **Travail/Emploi/Boulot** b. *Lawyer (F):* **Avocate** c. *Money*: **Argent** d. *Varied*: **Varié**
e. *Well-paid*: **Bien payé** f. *Sales assistant*: **Vendeur/Vendeuse** g. *Pleasant*: **Agréable**
h. *I will be*: **Je serai**
10. Guided translation
a. **Un emploi dans l'industrie** b. **Je voudrais devenir** c. **Un emploi en plein air**
d. **Je serai enseignant** e. **Car c'est agréable** f. **Je voudrais travailler comme**
g. **Je voudrais un emploi de bureau** h. **Un emploi dans le bénévolat**
11. English-to-French translation
a. Je voudrais travailler comme pilote car cela permet de voyager
b. Je voudrais travailler comme enseignant car cela est gratifiant
c. Je serai chirurgien car c'est un emploi bien payé
d. Je voudrais devenir avocat parce que c'est important
e. Je voudrais un emploi en plein air dans l'agriculture
f. Je voudrais travailler comme chauffeur de taxi car c'est varié

Unit 8. What job I would like to do and why - Higher - Answers

1. Match up

La vente – ***Sales*** Fatigant – ***Tiring*** En plein essor – ***Fast-growing*** Artisan – ***Craftsman***
Voyager – ***To travel*** Autres – ***Others*** Vendeur – ***Sales assistant*** Une fois – ***Once*** Comme – ***As***

2. Gapped translation

a. *After my **studies*** b. *In my **opinion*** c. ***According to** my friends* d. *My parents **tell** me*
e. *I **should** do* f. *I should **become*** g. *It's very **trendy***

3. Broken words

a. Les au**tres** b. Équi**pe** c. Cette car**rière** d. Une indus**trie** e. Choi**sir** f. La ven**te**

4. Faulty translation – Correct the wrong English translations

a. Les emplois de bureau: ***Office** jobs* b. Quant à moi: ***As for** me* c. Les travaux manuels: *Manual work* √
d. Je devrais travailler: *I should **work*** e. Mon frère me dit que: *My brother **tells me** that*
f. Mes profs pensent que: *My teachers **think** that* g. Un secteur en plein essor: *A fast-growing sector* √

5. Translate into English (all sections)

a. ***An independent job*** b. ***An office job*** c. ***As for me*** d. ***Fast-growing*** e. ***Tiring*** f. ***Outdoor***
g. ***My friends tell me that*** h. ***I should do medicine*** i. ***My teachers think that*** j. ***It seems demanding***
k. ***To work as a team*** l. ***A career in sales***

6. Missing vowels (jobs)

a. **avocat** b. **artisan** c. **comptable** d. **enseignant** e. **informaticien** f. **architecte**

7. Complete with the missing word

a. Un **travail** indépendant b. En **plein** essor c. Cela **semble** exigeant d. Je **voudrais** devenir artisan
e. Une carrière **dans** la vente f. Après **mes** études

8. Sentence puzzle

a. L'informatique, c'est un secteur fascinant et en plein essor
b. Quant à moi, je pense que je devrais devenir avocat
c. Après mes études, je voudrais travailler comme comptable
d. Mes amis disent que je devrais faire carrière dans la vente
e. Quant à moi je préfère les boulots de bureau
f. Mon frère me dit que je devrais travailler comme journaliste

9. Complete the table

Fast-growing: En plein essor *I would like to become*: **Je voudrais devenir**
Office jobs: Les boulots de bureau *According to me*: **Selon moi** ***As for me***: Quant à moi
My brother tells me that: Mon frère me dit que *Demanding*: **Exigeant**
To make a career: Faire carrière *A manual job*: **Un travail manuel**

10. Find in the wordsearch the French for the words listed in the box below

Tiring: **Fatigant** *Others*: **Autres** *Sales*: **Vente** *Sector*: **Secteur** *Craftsman*: **Artisan**
Job: **Boulot** *Industry*: **Industrie** *Office*: **Bureau** *Career*: **Carrière**

11. Guided translation

a. **En plein essor** b. **Selon moi** c. **Je voudrais devenir** d. **Un emploi de bureau**
e. **Je voudrais travailler** f. **Après mes études** g. **Dans la vente** h. **Cela me permettra**
i. **Instructeur de sport**

12. Translate into French

a. **Après mes études, je voudrais travailler comme chirurgien**
b. **J'aime ce travail car cela me permettra de voyager**
c. **Cela semble exigeant, mais pas stressant**
d. **Je devrais faire carrière dans la vente**
e. **Mes parents me disent que je devrais étudier la médecine**
f. **Mon frère me dit que je devrais travailler comme enseignant/professeur**
g. **Je préfère les boulots en plein air, donc je voudrais être agriculteur**
h. **Ce boulot me permettra d'aider les autres**
i. **Je rêve de cette carrière, car je pense que cette profession est fascinante**

UNIT 8 - Test - Answers (/100)

1. Vocabulary recognition - French-to-English translation (/15)

a. ***My studies***

b. ***To become***

c. ***Plumber***

d. ***I would like***

e. ***A job***

f. ***Tiring***

g. ***I will be***

h. ***Craftsman***

i. ***Office***

j. ***Outdoor***

k. ***To help***

l. ***Sales assistant***

m. ***Exciting***

n. ***It allows me to***

o. ***Well-paid***

2. Syntax/Lexicogrammar – Split sentences (/5)

Cela permet	**de voyager**
Je veux travailler	**dans le bénévolat**
Je voudrais un emploi	**en contact avec la nature**
À mon avis, c'est un	**secteur qui est assez lucratif**
Je voudrais un boulot en	**plein air**

3. Grammar/Morphology/Vocabulary – Tangled translation (/20)

a. Je **serai** plombier

b. Je **voudrais** un boulot **bien payé**

c. **Selon** mes **amis**

d. Je **veux** faire **ce boulot/travail**

e. Je voudrais avoir un boulot **en plein air**

f. Je voudrais **devenir** ingénieur

g. **Je préfère** le travail **indépendant**

h. C'est une **industrie qui est** lucrative

i. Je voudrais **travailler** comme **artisan**

j. Mes parents me **disent que (1)** je devrais être médecin

k. C'est très **tendance** en **ce** moment

l. Je voudrais faire une **carrière** dans la **vente**

4. Translate into French (/ 60 – each full sentence – 6 points)

a. **Une fois que je suis diplômé(e), je voudrais devenir comptable**

b. **J'aime cette profession car cela me permettra de (2) voyager**

c. **Mes parents me disent que je devrais étudier la médecine à l'université**

d. **Je préfère le travail indépendant, alors/donc je voudrais être artisan**

e. **Mes amis me disent que je devrais travailler comme instructeur de sport**

f. **Quant à moi, je préfère les boulots en plein air, alors/donc je pourrais être agriculteur**

g. **À mon avis, c'est un secteur qui est en plein essor en ce moment**

h. **Selon moi, c'est une industrie qui est assez lucrative aujourd'hui**

i. **Mon frère me dit que je devrais faire carrière dans le commerce**

j. **Après mes études, je voudrais travailler comme chirurgien parce que c'est un boulot bien payé**

Unit 9. Home, town, neighbourhood and region

KEY VOCABULARY Foundation

1. Les pièces *(rooms)*

Dans ma maison, il y a six pièces
In my house there are six rooms
-une cuisine: *a kitchen*
-un salon: *a living room*
-une salle à manger: *a dining room*
-des toilettes: *toilets*
-un garage: *a garage*
-un jardin: *a garden*
Au premier/deuxième étage, il y a:
On the first/second floor, there is/are
-quatre chambres: *four bedrooms*
-deux salles de bain: *two bathrooms*
-un bureau: *an office*

2. Les magasins (shops)

Dans ma ville/mon quartier, il y a:
In my town/neighbourhood there is/are
-des magasins: *shops*
-des centres commerciaux: *malls*
-une (grande) bibliothèque: *a (big) library*
-une gare: *a train station*
-une gare routière: *a bus station*
-des parcs: *parks*
-une zone piétonne: *a pedestrian area*
Dans ma rue, il y a...
In my street, there is...
-une boulangerie: *a bakery*
-une boucherie: *a butcher's*

3. Pourquoi j'aime/je n'aime pas ma ville/mon quartier

J'aime ma ville/mon quartier car c'est...
I like my town/neighbourhood as it's...
-joli: *pretty*
-propre: *clean*
-sûr: *safe*
-tranquille: *quiet*
Et il y a beaucoup/plein de choses à...
And there are lots of things to...
-faire: *do* / -voir: *see*
Je n'aime pas ma ville parce que c'est...
I don't like my town because it's...
-bruyant: *noisy*
-dangereux: *dangerous*
-pollué: *polluted*
-sale: *dirty*

1. Match

Il y a sept pièces	***On the first floor***
Dans ma ville	***In my neighbourhood***
Au premier étage	***On the second floor***
Dans mon quartier	***On my street***
Au deuxième étage	***In my town***
Dans ma rue	***Lots of things to do***
Plein de choses à voir	***Lots of things to see***
J'aime mon quartier	***I like my neighbourhood***
Plein de choses à faire	***There are seven rooms***

2. Gapped translation with options

a. Au ____________ étage: *On the second floor*
b. Il y a sept __________ : *There are 7 rooms*
c. Dans ________ maison: *In my house*
d. Plein de ________ à faire: *Lots of things to do*
e. Dans mon ____________ : *In my neighbourhood*
f. Au ____________ étage: *On the first floor*
g. Ma ville est __________ : *My town is polluted*
h. Ma rue est _________ : *My street is dirty*

choses	**polluée**	**pièces**	**premier**
quartier	**deuxième**	**ma**	**sale**

3. Broken words

a. Une ga_ _ : *A station*
b. Tran_ _ _ _ _ _ : *Quiet*
c. S_ _ : *Safe*
d. Cho_ _ _ : *Things*
e. Prop_ _ : *Clean*
f. Une bouche_ _ _ : *Butcher's*
g. Ru_ : *Street*
h. Bru_ _ _ _ : *Noisy*
i. Vo_ _ : *To see*
j. Sa_ _ : *Dirty*
k. Pol_ _ _ : *Polluted*
l. Jo_ _ : *Pretty*

4. Puzzle – Arrange the words in the correct order

a. zone Une piétonne grande: *A big pedestrian area*
b. aime ville J' ma: *I like my town*
c. de Plein faire choses à: *Lots of things to do*
d. pollué est C' assez: *It's quite polluted*
e. n' Ce pas est sûr: *It isn't safe*
f. premier Au étage: *On the first floor*
g. y Il a: *There is/are*
h. étage deuxième Au: *On the second floor*

5. Tick the adjectives and translate them into English

a. Grenier
b. Sale
c. Étage
d. Rue
e. Pollué
f. Joli
g. Quartier
h. Propre

6. Break the flow then translate into English

a. Dans/mon/appartement/il/y/a/sept/pièces: *In my flat there are 7 rooms*
b. Machambreestaupremierétage:
c. Jhabitedansunegrandemaison:
d. Jaimemonquartiercarilestpropreetsûr:
e. Malheureusementmavilleesttrèspolluée:
f. Dansmavilleilyaungrandcentrecommercial:
g. Jaimemonquartiercarilyabeaucoupdechosesàfaire:
h. Mavilleesttrèsbelleethistorique:
i. Dansmavilleilyapleindechosesàvoir:

7. Complete the sentences

a. Au p_______ étage: *On the first floor*
b. Dans ma v________ : *In my town*
c. Une s________ à manger: *A dining room*
d. D______ ma maison: *In my house*
e. Une zone p____________ : *A pedestrian area*
f. Il y a _______ parcs: *There are two parks*
g. Dans ____ rue: *In my street*
h. Dans mon quartier, il y a beaucoup ___ cafés
In my neighbourhood there are lots of cafés

8. Complete the table

English	French
In my street	
	Dans ma ville
	Il y a
On the second floor	
	Une rue piétonne
Lots of things to do	
	C'est bruyant
It is safe	
	C'est tranquille

9. Match the opposites

Propre	**Bruyant**
Grand	**Moche**
Sûr	**Sale**
Tranquille	**Nouveau**
Joli	**Petit**
Vieux	**Dangereux**

10. Translate the adjectives below into French

a. Dirty
b. Dangerous
c. Small
d. Ugly
e. Safe
f. Clean
g. Quiet
h. New

11. Tangled translation

a. J'habite **in** une vieille **house in** le centre-ville
b. Mon **neighbourhood** est **clean** et tranquille
c. Je n'**like** pas **my** ville, car c'est **noisy**
d. Dans ma **town**, il y a **lots of** choses à **do**
e. Mon quartier **is** assez **dirty** et **polluted**
f. **In** ma rue, **there is** un **big** centre commercial
g. J'**live** dans un petit **neighbourhood**
h. Au **first** étage, il y a trois **rooms**
i. **On the** deuxième **floor**, il y a quatre pièces

12. Translate into French

a. In my town, there are lots of things to do
b. On the second floor, there are five rooms
c. I live in a small house in the town centre
d. My neighbourhood is quite dirty and polluted
e. I don't like my town as it's noisy and dangerous
f. I like my neighbourhood a lot because it is clean
g. On the first floor, there are three rooms
h. In my town, there are lots of things to see
i. On my street, there are many cafés and shops

KEY VOCABULARY Higher

1. Les pièces de ma maison *(the rooms in my house)*

Chez moi... *At home...*
Au premier/deuxième étage... *On the first/second floor...*
...il y a: *there is/are...*
-sept pièces: *seven rooms*
-deux salles de bain: *two bathrooms*
-trois chambres: *three bedrooms*
-une cuisine: *a kitchen*
-un salon: *a living room*

2. Types de logement *(accommodation)*

J'habite dans... *I live in...*
-une maison: *a house*
-un appartement: *a flat*
-un immeuble: *a block of flats*

3. Là où j'habite *(where I live)*

-à la campagne: *in the countryside*
-à la montagne: *in the mountains*
-en banlieue: *on the outskirts*
-en ville: *in town*

4. Ce qu'il y a là où j'habite *(what there is where I live)*

Dans ma rue/mon quartier/ma ville/ma région il y a...
In my street/neighbourhood/town/region there is/are...
-des choses à faire/voir pour les jeunes *things to do/see for young people*
-des espaces verts: *green spaces*
-des magasins: *shops*
-des monuments/lieux historiques *historic monuments/places*
-des parcs d'attractions: *amusement parks*
-des plages: *beaches*
-des stations balnéaires: *seaside resorts*
-des stations de ski: *ski resorts*
-un centre commercial: *a mall*
-une bibliothèque: *a library*
-une rivière: *a river*
-une zone piétonne: *a pedestrian area*

5. Pourquoi j'aime/je n'aime pas mon quartier/ma ville

Car c'est... *As it's...*
-bruyant: *noisy* / -dangereux: *dangerous*
-joli: *pretty* / -moche: *ugly*
-propre *clean* / -sale: *dirty*
-tranquille: *quiet*
-sûr: *safe*

1. Match up

Magasins	***Block of flats***
Campagne	***Street***
Immeuble	***House***
Rue	***Floor***
Pièces	***Things***
Choses	***Town***
Banlieue	***Outskirts***
Ville	***Rooms***
Étage	***Shops***
Jeunes	***Countryside***
Maison	***Young people***

2. Gapped translation

a. J'habite en banlieue: *I live* ________________
b. Il y a six pièces: *There are six* ________________
c. Au premier étage: *On the* __________*floor*
d. Dans ma rue: *On my* __________
e. J'habite à la campagne: *I live in the* ____________
f. Dans mon quartier: *In my* ________________
g. Dans un immeuble moderne: *In a modern* _______
h. Où j'habite: ________ *I live*
i. Il y a des espaces verts: *There are* _______ *spaces*
j. Il y a de bons magasins: *There are* _______ *shops*

3. Translate into English

a. Des choses à faire

b. Des espaces verts

c. Dans ma rue

d. En banlieue

e. Au deuxième étage

f. Un vieil immeuble

g. Chez moi, il y a…

h. Une rue piétonne

4. Broken words

a. Cho_ _ : *Thing*
b. Ru_ : *Street*
c. Rivi_ _ _ : *River*
d. Pla_ _ : *Beach*
e. Pi_ _ _ _ : *Rooms*
f. Maga_ _ _ : *Shop*
g. Vi_ _ _ : *Town*
h. Cham_ _ _ : *Bedroom*

5. Missing vowels – Section 5 only

a. Br_y_nt
b. M_ch_
c. S_l_
d. S_r
e. J_l_
f. Pr_pr_
g. D_ng_r_ _x

6. Choose the correct translation

a. Campagne: *countryside / building / flat*

b. Immeuble: *block of flats / lake / river*

c. Étage: *outskirts / neighbourhood / floor*

d. Vieux: *new / old / ugly*

e. Banlieue: *outskirts / space / room*

f. Pièces: *streets / towns / rooms*

7. Complete with the correct option from the box

a. Une zone ____________

b. J'habite à la ___________

c. Chez ______

d. Des ________ à faire

e. Des _________ verts

f. Il y a huit _________

espaces
pièces
moi
choses
piétonne
campagne

8. Match the opposites

Joli	**Bruyant**
Vieux	**Sale**
Tranquille	**Moche**
Grand	**Pauvre**
Dangereux	**Nouveau**
Propre	**Petit**
Riche	**Sûr**

9. Gapped English-to-French translation

a. J'habite en _______ : *I live on the outskirts*

b. Dans ma _______ il y a des magasins: *On my street there are shops*

c. J'habite dans une _______ maison: *I live in an old house*

d. Mon __________ est bruyant: *My neighbourhood is noisy*

e. Au premier _______ il y a 3 pièces: *On the 1st floor there are 3 rooms*

f. Je n'aime pas ma _________ car elle est _______ et très petite:
I don't like my house because it is old and very small

g. Il __ a beaucoup de ____ historiques: *There are lots of historic places*

10. Complete the table

English	**Français**
Places	
	Quartier
	Pièces
Shops	
	Zone piétonne
Countryside	
	Moche
Clean	
Safe	

11. Find in the wordsearch the French for the words listed in the box below

S	D	Q	P	G	A	U	P
F	T	C	R	Q	E	Y	K
G	C	H	O	S	E	S	N
H	E	Q	P	L	A	G	E
I	S	O	R	F	É	M	L
S	A	L	E	H	T	B	B
U	P	R	E	D	A	Z	U
B	T	S	M	B	G	C	E
V	P	I	È	C	E	S	M
X	H	L	F	R	E	A	M
B	R	U	Y	A	N	T	I

Rooms: P

Things: C

Dirty: S

Beach: P

Floor: É

Noisy: B

Block of flats: I

Clean: P

12. Guided translation

a. *My town is clean*: M_ v____ e___ p_______

b. *My neighbourhood*: M___ q__________

c. *There are sea resorts*: I_ y a d___ st_________
b__________

d. *I live on the outskirts*: J'h_____ e_ b________

e. *It's safe, but noisy*: C'e__ s___, m___ b______

f. *Many green spaces*: B______ d'e______ v___

g. *A pedestrian area*: U___ z___ p___________

h. *My town is not safe*: M_ v____ n'est pas s____

i. *At home there are seven rooms*:
C_____ m_____ i_ y a s_____ p________

j. *Things to visit*: D__ c______ à v___________

13. Translate into French

a. My town is dirty and polluted

b. I live in an old block of flats

c. In my house, there are eight rooms

d. My neighbourhood is very noisy

e. In my region, there are many ski resorts

f. I live in a small house in the mountains

g. In my town, there are many green spaces

h. My neighbourhood is clean and safe

UNIT 9 - Test (/100)

1. Vocabulary recognition: French-to-English translation (/15)

a. Dans ma maison
b. Au premier étage
c. Une salle à manger
d. Il y a
e. Au deuxième étage
f. Des choses à faire
g. Dans mon quartier
h. Sept pièces
i. Des chose à voir
j. Dans ma ville
k. Dans ma rue
l. C'est propre
m. C'est bruyant
n. C'est dangereux
o. C'est sale

2. Syntax/Lexicogrammar – Split sentences (/5)

Au premier étage il y	magasins dans ma rue
J'habite à	à faire
Il n' y a pas de	a quatre pièces
Il y a plein de choses	c'est assez joli
J'aime ma ville car	la campagne

3. Grammar/Morphology/Vocabulary – Tangled translation (/20)

a. **There are** des espaces **green**
b. Dans ma ville, il n'y pas de zone **pedestrian**
c. Au premier **floor**, il y a ma chambre
d. Dans my **street**, il n'y a pas de **bakery**
e. J'habite dans une **old house** en banlieue
f. Il y a beaucoup de **places historic**
g. Dans ma région, il y a plein de choses **to do**
h. **At home**, il y a huit **rooms**
i. Mon **neighbourhood** est assez propre **and pretty**
j. Le centre-ville est très **noisy** and **polluted**
k. Ce que j'aime le plus, ce sont les **shops**
l. Mon quartier est **safe** et **quiet**

4. Translate into French (/ 60 – each full sentence – 6 points)

a. What I like the most in my town, it's the shopping mall
b. I don't like my neighbourhood because it's dirty and dangerous
c. I would like to live in the countryside because it's less polluted
d. In my neighbourhood, there are not many things to do
e. In the town centre there are many shops and cafés
f. In my street, there is a bakery, a supermarket and a gym
g. I hate my town because it's ugly and noisy
h. I live in a small flat in an old block of flats on the outskirts
i. In my house, there are five rooms. My favourite room is my bedroom
j. Unfortunately, there isn't an airport or a swimming pool in my town

Unit 9. Home, town, neighbourhood and region - Foundation - Answers

1. Match
Il y a sept pièces – ***There are seven rooms*** Dans ma ville – ***In my town***
Au premier étage – ***On the first floor*** Dans mon quartier – ***In my neighbourhood***
Au deuxième étage – ***On the second floor*** Dans ma rue – ***On my street***
Plein de choses à voir – ***Lots of things to see*** J'aime mon quartier – ***I like my neighbourhood***
Plein de choses à faire – ***Lots of things to do***
2. Gapped translation with options
a. Au **deuxième** étage b. Il y a sept **pièces** c. Dans **ma** maison d. Plein de **choses** à faire
e. Dans mon **quartier** f. Au **premier** étage g. Ma ville est **polluée** h. Ma rue est **sale**
3. Broken words
a. Une ga**re** b. Tran**quille** c. S**ûr** d. Ch**oses** e. Prop**re** f. Une bouche**rie** g. R**ue**
h. Bru**yant** i. Vo**ir** j. Sa**le** k. Poll**ué** l. Jo**li**
4. Puzzle – arrange the words in the correct order
a. **Une grande zone piétonne** b. **J'aime ma ville** c. **Plein de choses à faire** d. **C'est assez pollué**
e. **Ce n'est pas sûr** f. **Au premier étage** g. **Il y a** h. **Au deuxième étage**
5. Tick the adjectives and translate them into English
a. Grenier b. **Sale:** ***Dirty*** c. Étage d. Rue f. **Joli:** ***Pretty*** g. Quartier h. **Propre:** ***Clean***
6. Break the flow then translate into English
a. *Example*: Dans/mon/appartement/il/y/a/sept/pièces: *In my flat there are 7 rooms*
b. **Ma chambre est au premier étage:** ***My bedroom is on the first floor***
c. **J'habite dans une grande maison:** ***I live in a big house***
d. **J'aime mon quartier car il est propre et sûr:** ***I like my neighbourhood as it's clean and safe***
e. **Malheureusement ma ville est très polluée:** ***Unfortunately my town is very polluted***
f. **Dans ma ville il y a un grand centre commercial:** ***In my town, there is a big mall***
g. **J'aime mon quartier car il y a beaucoup de choses à faire:**
I like my neighbourhood as there are lots of things to do
h. **Ma ville est très belle et historique:** ***My town is very beautiful and historic***
i. **Dans ma ville il y a plein de choses à voir:** ***In my town, there are lots of things to see***
7. Complete the sentences
a. Au **premier** étage b. Dans ma **ville** c. Une **salle** à manger d. **Dans** ma maison e. Une zone **piétonne**
f. Il y a **deux** parcs g. Dans **ma** rue h. Dans mon quartier, il y a beaucoup **de** cafés
8. Complete the table
In my street: **Dans ma rue** ***In my town***: Dans ma ville ***There is/are***: Il y a
On the second floor: **Au deuxième étage** ***A pedestrian street***: Une rue piétonne
Lots of things to do: **Plein de choses à faire** ***It is noisy***: C'est bruyant *It is safe*: **C'est sûr**
It is quiet: C'est tranquille
9. Match the opposites
Propre: **Sale** Grand: **Petit** Sûr: **Dangereux** Tranquille: **Bruyant** Joli: **Moche** Vieux: **Nouveau**
10. Translate the adjectives below into French
a. *Dirty*: **Sale** b. *Dangerous*: **Dangereux** c. *Small*: **Petit** d. *Ugly*: **Moche** e. *Safe*: **Sûr**
f. *Clean*: **Propre** g. *Quiet*: ***Tranquille*** h. *New*: **Nouveau**
11. Tangled translation
a. J'habite **dans** une vieille **maison dans** le centre-ville b. Mon **quartier** est **propre** et tranquille
c. Je n'**aime** pas **ma** ville, car c'est **bruyant** d. Dans ma **ville**, il y a **beaucoup de/plein de** choses à **faire**
e. Mon quartier **est** assez **sale** et **pollué** f. **Dans** ma rue, **il y a** un **grand** centre commercial
g. J'**habite** dans un petit **quartier** h. Au **premier** étage, il y a trois **pièces**
i. **Au** deuxième **étage**, il y a quatre pièces
12. Translate into French
a. **Dans ma ville, il y a beaucoup de choses à faire** b. **Au deuxième étage, il y a cinq pièces**
c. **J'habite dans une petite maison en centre-ville** d. **Mon quartier est assez sale et pollué**
e. **Je n'aime pas ma ville, car c'est bruyant et dangereux**
f. **J'aime beaucoup mon quartier parce que c'est propre** g. **Au premier étage, il y a trois pièces**
h. **Dans ma ville, il y a plein de choses à voir** i. **Dans ma rue, il y a beaucoup de cafés et de magasins**

Unit 9. Home, town, neighbourhood and region - Higher - Answers

1. Match up

Magasins – ***Shops*** Campagne – ***Countryside*** Immeuble – ***Block of flats*** Rue – ***Street***
Pièces – ***Rooms*** Choses – ***Things*** Banlieue – ***Outskirts*** Ville – ***Town*** Étage – ***Floor***
Jeunes – ***Young people*** Maison – ***House***

2. Gapped translation

a. J'habite en banlieue: *I live **on the outskits*** b. Il y a six pièces: *There are six **rooms***
c. Au premier étage: *On the **first** floor* d. Dans ma rue: *On my **street***
e. J'habite à la campagne: *I live in the **countryside*** f. Dans mon quartier: *In my **neighbourhood***
g. Dans un immeuble moderne: *In a modern **block of flats*** h. Où j'habite: ***Where** I live*
i. Il y a des espaces verts: *There are **green** spaces* j. Il y a de bons magasins: *There are **good** shops*

3. Translate into English

a. ***Things to do*** b. ***Green spaces*** c. ***On my street*** d. ***On the outskits*** e. ***On the second floor***
f. ***An old block of flats*** g. ***At home, there is/are...*** h. ***A pedestrian street***

4. Broken words

a. Ch**ose**: *Thing* b. R**ue**: *Street* c. Rivi**ère**: *River* d. Pla**ge**: *Beach* e. Pi**èces**: *Rooms*
f. Maga**sin** : *Shop* g.Vi**lle**: *Town* h. Cham**bre**: *Bedroom*

5. Missing vowels – Section 5 only

a. **Bruyant** b. **Moche** c. **Sale** d. **Sûr** e. **Joli** f. **Propre** g. **Dangereux**

6. Choose the correct translation

a. Campagne: ***countryside*** b. Immeuble: ***block of flats*** c. Étage: ***floor***
d. Vieux: ***old*** e. Banlieue: ***outskirts*** f. Pièces: ***rooms***

7. Complete with the correct option from the box

a. Une zone **piétonne** b. J'habite à la **campagne** c. Chez **moi** d. Des **choses** à faire
e. Des **espaces** verts f. Il y a huit **pièces**

8. Match the opposites

Joli: **Moche** Vieux: **Nouveau** Tranquille: **Bruyant** Grand: **Petit** Dangereux: **Sûr**
Propre: **Sale** Riche: **Pauvre**

9. Gapped English-to-French translation

a. J'habite en **banlieue** b. Dans ma **rue**, il y a des magasins c. J'habite dans une **vieille** maison
d. Mon **quartier** est bruyant e. Au premier **étage**, il y a 3 pièces
f. Je n'aime pas ma **maison** car elle est **vieille** et très petite g. Il **y** a beaucoup de **lieux** historiques

10. Complete the table

Places: **Lieux** ***Neighbourhood***: Quartier ***Rooms***: Pièces *Shops*: **Magasins**
Pedestrian area: Zone piétonne *Countryside*: **Campagne** ***Ugly***: Moche *Clean*: **Propre** *Safe*: **Sûr**

11. Find in the wordsearch the French for the words listed in the box below

Rooms: **Pièces** *Things*: **Choses** *Dirty*: **Sale** *Beach*: **Plage** *Floor*: **Étage**
Noisy: **Bruyant** *Block of flats*: **Immeuble** *Clean*: **Propre**

12. Guided translation

a. **Ma ville est propre** b. **Mon quartier** c. **Il y a des stations balnéaires** d. **J'habite en banlieue**
e. **C'est sûr, mais bruyant** f. **Beaucoup d'espaces verts** g. **Une zone piétonne**
h. **Ma ville n'est pas sûre** i. **Chez moi, il y a sept pièces** j. **Des choses à visiter**

13. Translate into French

a. Ma ville est sale et polluée b. J'habite dans un vieil immeuble c. Dans ma maison, il y a huit pièces
d. Mon quartier est très bruyant e. Dans ma région, il y a beaucoup de stations de ski
f. J'habite dans une petite maison à la montagne g. Dans ma ville, il y a beaucoup d'espaces verts
h. Mon quartier est propre et sûr

UNIT 9 - Test - Answers (/100)

1. Vocabulary recognition - French-to-English translation (/15)

a. ***In my house***

b. ***On the first floor***

c. ***A dining room***

d. ***There is/are***

e. ***On the second floor***

f. ***Things to do***

g. ***In my neighbourhood***

h. ***Seven rooms***

i. ***Things to see***

j. ***In my town***

k. ***In my street***

l. ***It's clean***

m. ***It's noisy***

n. ***It's dangerous***

o. ***It's dirty***

2. Syntax/Lexicogrammar – Split sentences (/5)

Au premier étage il y	**a quatre pièces**
J'habite à	**la campagne**
Il n' y a pas de	**magasins dans ma rue**
Il y a plein de choses	**à faire**
J'aime ma ville car	**c'est assez joli**

3. Grammar/Morphology/Vocabulary – Tangled translation (/20)

a. **Il y a** des espaces **verts**

b. Dans ma ville, il n'y pas de zone **piétonne**

c. Au premier **étage**, il y a ma chambre

d. Dans my **rue**, il n'y a pas de **boulangerie**

e. J'habite dans une **vieille** **maison** en banlieue

f. Il y a beaucoup de **lieux** **historiques**

g. Dans ma région, il y a plein de choses **à faire**

h. **Chez moi**, il y a huit **pièces**

i. Mon **quartier** est assez propre **et joli**

j. Le centre-ville est très **bruyant** and **pollué**

k. Ce que j'aime le plus, ce sont les **magasins**

l. Mon quartier est **sûr** et **tranquille**

4. Translate into French (/ 60 – each full sentence – 6 points)

a. **Ce que j'aime le plus (2) dans ma ville, c'est le centre commercial**

b. **Je n'aime pas mon quartier parce que c'est sale et dangereux**

c. **Je voudrais habiter/vivre à la campagne parce que c'est moins pollué**

d. **Dans mon quartier, il n'y a pas beaucoup de choses à faire**

e. **Dans le centre-ville, il y a beaucoup de magasins et de cafés**

f. **Dans ma rue, il y a une boulangerie, un supermarché et un gymnase**

g. **Je déteste ma ville parce que c'est moche et bruyant**

h. **J'habite dans un petit appartement dans un vieil immeuble en banlieue**

i. **Dans ma maison, il y a cinq pièces. Ma pièce préférée est ma chambre**

j. **Malheureusement, il n'y a pas d' aéroport ou de piscine dans ma ville**

Unit 10. Travel and tourism

KEY VOCABULARY Foundation

1. Les pays *(countries)*
L'année dernière, je suis allé(e) en...
Last year I went to...
L'année prochaine, j'irai en...
Next year, I will go to...
-Allemagne: *Germany*
-Angleterre: *England*
-Écosse: *Scotland*
-Espagne: *Spain*

2. Les transports
J'ai voyagé en... *I travelled by...*
Je voyagerai en... *I will travel by...*
-avion: *plane*
-bateau: *boat*
-voiture: *car*

3. Les logements *(accommodation)*
J'ai logé dans... *I stayed in...*
Je logerai dans... *I will stay in...*
-une auberge de jeunesse: *a youth hostel*
-un camping: *a campsite*
-un hôtel (quatre étoiles): *a (4-star) hotel*

4. Les endroits à visiter *(places to visit)*
J'ai visité... *I visited...*
Je visiterai... *I will visit...*
-des châteaux: *castles*
-des lieux historiques: *historic places*
-des musées: *museums*

5. Les endroits où aller *(places to go)*
Je suis allé(e)... *I went...*
J'irai... *I will go...*
-à la plage: *to the beach*
-au parc d'attractions: *to the theme park*
-au restaurant: *to the restaurant*
-en boîte: *clubbing*

6. Les activités à faire *(activities to do)*
J'ai fait... *I did...*
Je ferai... *I will do...*
-du kayak: *kayaking*
-du tourisme: *some sightseeing*
-de la plongée: *scuba diving*
-des visites guidées: *guided visits*

7. Les adjectifs utiles
C'était... *It was...*
Ce sera... *It will be...*
-amusant: *fun* / -génial: *great*
-inoubliable: *unforgettable*
-relaxant: *relaxing*

1. Match

En avion	***England***
Allemagne	***By car***
Une auberge de jeunesse	***Germany***
Angleterre	***A youth hostel***
En bateau	***To the beach***
Écosse	***Unforgettable***
À la plage	***By plane***
En voiture	***Greece***
Inoubliable	***Scotland***
Grèce	***By boat***

2. Gapped translation

a. L'année dernière: *Last* ______
b. En Allemagne: *In* ___________
c. J'ai logé dans: *I* ________ *in*
d. En avion: *By* ________
e. Des lieux historiques: *Historic* _________
f. Un hôtel trois étoiles: *A* ___________ *hotel*
g. Je suis allé en boîte: *I went* _____________
h. J'ai fait de la plongée: *I went* ______________

3. Broken words

a. J'ai lo_ _ : *I stayed*
b. Dans un camp_ _ _ : *In a campsite*
c. Je suis allé en bo_ _ _ : *I went clubbing*
d. Je loge_ _ _ : *I will stay*
e. À la pla_ _ : *To the beach*
f. Je fe_ _ _ : *I will do*
g. La plon_ _ _ : *Scuba diving*

4. Break the flow

a. Jiraiàlaplagetouslesjours
b. Jeferaidelaplongéeetdukayak
c. Ceserainoubliable
d. Jevisiteraideslieuxhistoriques
e. LannéedernièrejesuisalléenGrèce
f. LannéeprochainejiraienItalie
g. Jaivoyagéenavionetpuisenvoiture

5. Missing vowels

a. B_ _t_: *Club*
b. Pl_ng_ _: *Scuba diving*
c. G_n_ _l: *Great*
d. T_ _r_sm_: *Tourism*
e. _m_s_nt: *Fun*
f. R_l_x_nt: *Relaxing*
g. J_f_r_ _: *I will do*
h. L_ _ _x: *Places*
i. Ch_t_ _ _x: *Castles*

6. Complete the table

Perfect tense	Present	Future
	Je vais	
		Je ferai
	Je voyage	
J'ai visité		
(Imperfect)	C'est	
		Je logerai
J'ai mangé		
	J'achète	
		Je prendrai

7. Gapped English-to-French translation

a. Je __________ en avion: *I will travel by plane*

b. J'___________ de la plongée: *I did scuba diving*

c. Je suis allé en _________ : *I went clubbing*

d. J'ai _________ des plats locaux: *I ate local dishes*

e. J'ai logé dans un hôtel quatre ___________ :
I stayed in a four-star hotel

f. J'____________ en train: *I travelled by train*

g. Ce _______ génial: *It will be great*

h. J'________ à la plage: *I will go to the beach*

i. C'était _____________ : *It was unforgettable*

j. Je suis allé en __________ : *I went to Scotland*

8. Complete the table

English	French
Four-star hotel	
I will go	
	C'était inoubliable
It will be great	
	Je voyagerai
Scotland	
	J'ai fait du tourisme

9. Find in the wordsearch the French for the words listed in the box below

C	H	Â	T	E	A	U	X
E	T	U	O	C	P	S	F
P	H	G	M	Y	L	P	I
L	J	È	R	P	A	N	A
O	G	N	U	B	G	M	R
N	N	I	S	O	E	V	I
G	I	A	T	Î	U	B	J'
É	P	L	S	T	K	S	C
E	M	H	F	E	I	X	G
Y	A	V	I	O	N	H	Q
É	C	O	S	S	E	U	T

Castles: C
Beach: P
Scuba diving: P
Great: G
Club: B
I will go: J'i
Campsite: C
Scotland: É
Plane: A

10. Complete

a. L'année p_________, j'irai e__ Écosse

b. Je v_____________ en avion et puis e__ voiture

c. Je l_________ dans un hôtel quatre é_________

d. Je f________ du tourisme et je p___________ beaucoup de photos

e. Je m_____________ au restaurant, j'a__________ des vêtements
et je v____________ des musées, des ch_________ et une cathédrale

f. Ce s________ génial!

11. Translate into French

a. I will eat
b. It was unforgettable
c. I will go
d. I will visit
e. I will be
f. It will be great
g. I will go clubbing

12. Translate into French

a. Last year, I went to Spain
b. I travelled by plane and then by car
c. Next year, I will go to France
d. I will travel by train, then by boat
e. I will stay in a youth hostel
f. I will take a lot of photos
g. I will do some sightseeing
h. I visited a lot of historic places
i. It was relaxing and unforgettable
j. I stayed in a four-star hotel
k. I did swimming and scuba diving
l. Next summer, I will stay in campsite
m. I will eat local food
n. I will go to the beach, it will be great!

KEY VOCABULARY Higher

1. Les pays que j'ai visité et visiterai

Je suis allé/J'irai… *I went/I will go...*
-au Portugal: *to Portugal*
-aux États-Unis: *to the United States*
-en Allemagne: *to Germany*

2. Comment j'ai voyagé et voyagerai

J'ai voyagé/Je voyagerai…
I travelled/I will travel...
-à vélo: *by bike*
-en avion: *by plane*
-en car: *by coach*
J'ai loué/Je louerai… *I rented/I will rent...*
-un vélo: *a bike* / -une voiture: *a car*

3. Où j'ai passé mes vacances

J'ai logé/Je logerai dans…
I stayed/I will stay in...
-une auberge de jeunesse: *a youth hostel*
-un hôtel trois/quatre/cinq étoiles
a 3/4/5-star hotel
-au bord de la mer: *by the sea*
-à la campagne: *in the countryside*
-à la montagne: *in the mountains*

4. Combien de temps j'y suis resté/Je vais y rester

J'ai passé/Je passerai… *I spent/I will spend...*
-cinq jours: *five days*
-une semaine: *one week*
-tout l'été: *all summer*

5. Pour mes activités

Le matin... *In the morning...*
L'après-midi... *In the afternoon...*
Le soir... *In the evening...*
Tous les jours... *Every day...*
J'ai fait/Je ferai… *I did/I will do...*
-de la natation: *swimming*
-de la plongée: *scuba diving*
-des visites guidées: *guided visits*
-du tourisme: *sightseeing*
-les magasins: *shopping*
J'ai mangé/Je mangerai au restaurant
I ate/I will eat at the restaurant
Je suis sorti(e)/Je sortirai
I went out/I will go out
Je suis allé(e) en boîte: *I went clubbing*
J'ai visité/Je visiterai
I visited/I will visit
-des lieux historiques/connus:
historic/well-known places

6. Comment c'était/ce sera

C'était/Ce sera… *It was/It will be...*
-génial: *great* / -intéressant: *interesting*
-nul: *rubbish*
-relaxant: *relaxing*

1. Match

En été	***Stars***
J'irai	***In the winter***
En hiver	***I will rent***
Le matin	***A week***
Une semaine	***In the countryside***
Je passerai	***I spent***
Étoiles	***I rented***
J'ai loué	***In the morning***
Je suis allé	***I will go***
À la campagne	***I went***
J'ai passé	***I will spend***
Je louerai	***In the summer***

2. Gapped translation

a. J'irai à la campagne: *I will go to the* ____________
b. Au bord de la mer: *By the* ________
c. Un hôtel quatre étoiles: *A* ___________ *hotel*
d. J'ai fait de la natation: *I* _______________
e. Je ferai de la plongée: *I will do* ____________
f. J'ai loué un vélo: *I* __________ *a bike*
g. J'y ai passé une semaine: *I spent* ___________ *there*
h. Je suis allé en boîte: *I went* _____________
i. Le soir, je suis sorti: *In the evening, I*_____________
j. Je voyagerai en voiture: *I* _______________ *by car*

3. Translate into English

a. J'ai fait les magasins

b. J'ai passé tout l'été en France

c. J'ai logé dans une auberge de jeunesse

d. J'ai visité des lieux historiques

e. Ce sera génial

f. C'était au bord de la mer

g. J'ai fait du tourisme

h. J'ai pris des photos

4. Broken words

a. Mat_ _ : *Morning*
b. Ét_ : *Summer*
c. Plon_ _ _ : *Diving*
d. Pla_ _ : *Beach*
e. Jo_ _ _ : *Days*
f. Maga_ _ _ _ : *Shops*
g. N_ _ : *Rubbish*
h. Li_ _ _ : *Places*

5. Missing vowels (section 5 and 6)

a. L_ _ _x h_st_r_qu_s
b. M_g_s_ns
c. G_n_ _l
d. Pl_ng_ _
e. C_nn_s
f. N_l
g. Je s_rt_r_ _

6. Choose the correct translation

a. Campagne: *countryside / week / plane*

b. Passer: *to spend / to rent / to stay*

c. Lieux: *stars / places / swimming*

d. Louer: *to spend / to stay / to rent*

e. Étoiles: *youngsters / stars / visits*

f. Loger: *to go / to stay / to rent*

7. Complete with the correct option from the box

a. J'y passerai une __________

b. J'ai fait de la __________

c. Une auberge de __________

d. Je voyagerai en __________

e. J'ai fait des visites __________

f. J'ai fait du __________

tourisme
plongée
jeunesse
voiture
guidées
semaine

8. Break the flow

a. LannéedernièrejesuisalléauPortugal

b. Jaivoyagéenavionpuisjailouéunevoiture

c. Jailogédansunhôtelauborddelamer

d. Lematinjesuisalléeàlaplage.Cétaitrelaxant

e. Àmidijaimangéaurestaurantdelhôtel

f. Laprès-midijaifaitdelavoileetdelaplongée

g. Jaiaussifaitlesmagasinsetdutourisme

h. Lesoirjesuissortiavecmonfrèreaîné

9. Split sentences

Je suis allée en	**une semaine**
J'ai logé	**lieux historiques**
J'y ai passé	**Allemagne**
J'ai fait de	**dans un hôtel**
Je suis allé au	**la natation**
J'ai visité des	**tourisme**
J'ai fait du	**Portugal**

10. Complete the table

Français	English
	I will rent
J'ai loué	
	I will spend
J'ai passé	
	I stayed
Je vais visiter	
	I did
Je ferai	
	I will visit

11. Find in the wordsearch the French for the words listed in the box below

P	S	P	L	O	U	E	R
A	D	L	T	U	V	A	S
S	S	O	I	R	O	H	F
S	F	N	U	P	I	J	C
E	B	G	S	M	T	Z	L
R	J	É	T	R	U	V	A
L	M	E	Q	A	R	M	I
L	I	E	U	X	E	I	N
T	U	O	R	E	Y	R	É
A	D	K	P	Q	J	O	G
C	A	M	P	A	G	N	E

Diving: P

Evening: S

Places: L

To rent: L

Car: V

Countryside: C

Great: G

To spend: P

12. Guided translation

a. *In the morning*: L_ m_ _ _ _

b. *I went clubbing*: J_ s_ _ _ a_ _ _ e_ b_ _ _ _

c. *Historic places*: L_ _ _ _ h_ _ _ _ _ _ _ _ _ _

d. *I did sightseeing*: J'_ _ f_ _ _ d_ t_ _ _ _ _ _ _

e. *I spent a week*: J'_ _ p_ _ _ _ u_ _ s_ _ _ _ _ _

f. *I will visit*: J_ v_ _ _ _ _ _ _ _

g. *By the sea*: A_ b_ _ _ d_ l_ m_ _

h. *I will swim*: J_ f_ _ _ _ d_ l_ n_ _ _ _ _ _ _

i. *It will be great*: C_ s_ _ _ g_ _ _ _ _

j. *It will be relaxing*: C_ s_ _ _ r_ _ _ _ _ _ _

k. *I will spend*: J_ p_ _ _ _ _ _ _

l. *I will go to Spain*: J'i_ _ _ e_ E_ _ _ _ _ _

13. Translate into French

a. I stayed in a three-star hotel by the sea

b. I travelled by train and then I rented a car

c. In the morning, I went to the beach and afterwards I did some sightseeing

d. I visited a lot of historic places and museums

e. I will do scuba diving. It will be great!

f. I will spend two weeks in Spain

g. It was very interesting and relaxing

h. In the evening, I went clubbing with my older brother

UNIT 10 - Test (/100)

1. Vocabulary recognition: French-to-English translation (/15)

a. Je voyagerai

b. Allemagne

c. Ensuite

d. Je passerai

e. Une auberge de jeunesse

f. J'ai voyagé

g. En avion

h. Une voiture

i. Au bord de la mer

j. Jours

k. Pendant

l. Cette année

m. En été

n. À la campagne

o. En voiture

2. Syntax/Lexicogrammar – Split sentences (/5)

Tous les jours j'ai fait	la plage
J'ai mangé	de lieux historiques
J'ai bronzé (sunbathed) à	des visites guidées
Il y avait beaucoup	dans une auberge de jeunesse
J'ai logé	au restaurant

3. Grammar/Morphology/Vocabulary – Tangled translation (/20)

a. J'ai passé deux **weeks** en **Germany**

b. J'ai **visited** des **places** historiques

c. C'était très **interesting**

d. **In the afternoon**, j'ai **sunbathed** à la plage

e. C'était **really** amusant et **relaxing**

f. Je **will spend** cinq jours à la **countryside**

g. **During** les **holidays**, je suis allé en Grèce

h. À christmas, j'**will go** en France

i. Ce **will be** génial!

j. Le soir, **I went out** avec mes amis

k. Je **will stay** dans un hôtel quatre **stars**

l. Je **will do** de la **scuba diving**

4. Translate into French (/ 60 – each full sentence – 6 points)

a. Last year, in the summer, I went to Spain

b. I travelled by plane and then I rented a car

c. We stayed in a five-star hotel by the sea

d. We spent one week in Portugal. It was fun!

e. I did some sightseeing and I took many pictures

f. There were many things to do and many places to see

g. Next year, I will go to Germany. I will travel by plane

h. I will stay in a youth hostel in Berlin

i. I will visit historic places and well-known monuments. It will be great!

j. This summer, I will go to Scotland and I will travel by car and then I will rent a bike

Unit 10. Travel and tourism - Foundation - Answers

1. Match

En avion – ***By plane*** Allemagne – ***Germany*** Une auberge de jeunesse – ***A youth hostel***
Angleterre – ***England*** En bateau – ***By boat*** Écosse – ***Scotland*** À la plage – ***To the beach***
En voiture – ***By car*** Inoubliable – ***Unforgettable*** Grèce – ***Greece***

2. Gapped translation

a. *Last* ***year*** b. *In* ***Germany*** c. *I* ***stayed*** *in* d. *By* ***plane*** e. *Historic* ***places***
f. *A* ***3-star*** *hotel* g. *I went* ***clubbing*** h. *I went* ***scuba diving***

3. Broken words

a. J'ai log**é** b. Dans un camp**ing** c. Je suis allé en bo**îte** d. Je loger**ai** e. À la pla**ge**
f. Je fer**ai** g. La plong**ée**

4. Break the flow

a. J'irai à la plage tous les jours b. Je ferai de la plongée et du kayak c. Ce sera inoubliable
d. Je visiterai des lieux historiques e. L'année dernière je suis allé en Grèce
f. L'année prochaine j'irai en Italie g. J'ai voyagé en avion et puis en voiture

5. Missing vowels

a. **Boîte** b. **Plongée** c. **Génial** d. **Tourisme** e. **Amusant** f. **Relaxant**
g. **Je ferai** h. **Lieux** i. **Châteaux**

6. Complete the table

Je suis allé(e)/ Je vais/ **J'irai** **J'ai fait/ Je fais/** Je ferai **J'ai voyagé/** Je voyage/ **Je voyagerai**
J'ai visité/ **Je visite/ Je visiterai** **C'était/** C'est/ **Ce sera** **J'ai logé/Je loge/** Je logerai
J'ai mangé/ **Je mange/ Je mangerai** **J'ai acheté/** J'achète/ **J'achèterai** **J'ai pris/ Je prends/** Je prendrai

7. Gapped English-to-French translation

a. Je **voyagerai** en avion b. **J'ai fait** de la plongée c. Je suis allé en **boîte** d. J'ai **mangé** des plats locaux
e. J'ai logé dans un hôtel quatre **étoiles** f. J'**ai voyagé** en train g. Ce **sera** génial h. J'**irai** à la plage
i. C'était **inoubliable** j. Je suis allé en **Écosse**

8. Complete the table

Four-star hotel: **Hôtel quatre étoiles** *I will go*: **J'irai** ***It was unforgettable***: C'était inoubliable
It will be great: **Ce sera génial** ***I will travel***: Je voyagerai *Scotland*: **Écosse**
I did some sightseeing: J'ai fait du tourisme

9. Find in the wordsearch the French for the words listed in the box below

Castles: **Châteaux** *Beach*: **Plage** *Scuba diving*: **Plongée** *Great*: **Génial** *Club*: **Boîte**
I will go: **J'irai** *Campsite*: **Camping** *Scotland*: **Écosse** *Plane*: **Avion**

10. Complete

a. L'année **prochaine**, j'irai **en** Écosse b. Je **voyagerai** en avion et puis **en** voiture
c. Je **logerai** dans un hôtel quatre **étoiles** d. Je **ferai** du tourisme et je **prendrai** beaucoup de photos
e. Je **mangerai** au restaurant, **j'achèterai** des vêtements et je **visiterai** des musées, des **châteaux** et une cathédrale f. Ce **sera** génial!

11. Translate into French

a. **Je mangerai** b. **C'était inoubliable** c. **J'irai** d. **Je visiterai** e. **Je serai**
f. **Ce sera génial** g. **J'irai en boîte**

12. Translate into French

a. **L'année dernière, je suis allé(e) en Espagne**
b. **J'ai voyagé en avion et puis en voiture**
c. **L'année prochaine, j'irai en France**
d. **Je voyagerai en train, puis en bateau**
e. **Je logerai dans une auberge de jeunesse**
f. **Je prendrai beaucoup de photos**
g. **Je ferai du tourisme**
h. **J'ai visité beaucoup de lieux historiques**
i. **C'était relaxant et inoubliable**
j. **J'ai logé dans un hôtel quatre étoiles**
k. **J'ai fait de la natation et de la plongée**
l. **L'été prochain je logerai dans un camping**
m. **Je mangerai de la nourriture locale**
n. **J'irai à la plage, ce sera génial!**

Unit 10. Travel and tourism - Higher - Answers

1. Match

En été – ***In the summer*** J'irai – ***I will go*** En hiver – ***In the winter*** Le matin – ***In the morning***
Une semaine – ***A week*** Je passerai – ***I will spend*** Étoiles – ***Stars*** J'ai loué – ***I rented***
Je suis allé – ***I went*** À la campagne – ***In the countryside*** J'ai passé – ***I spent*** Je louerai – ***I will rent***

2. Gapped translation

a. *I will go to the* ***countryside*** b. *By the* ***sea*** c. *A* ***4-star*** *hotel* d. *I* ***did swimming*** e. *I will do* ***scuba diving***
f. *I* ***rented*** *a bike* g. *I spent* ***a week*** *there* h. *I went* ***clubbing*** i. *In the evening, I* ***went out***
j. *I* ***will travel*** *by car*

3. Translate into English

a. ***I did/went shopping*** b. ***I spent all summer in France*** c. ***I stayed in a youth hostel***
d. ***I visited historic places*** e. ***It will be great*** f. ***It was by the sea*** g. ***I did some sightseeing***
h. ***I took some photos***

4. Broken words

a. Mat**in** b. **Été** c. Plong**ée** d. Pla**ge** e. Jo**urs** f. Maga**sins** g. N**ul** h. Lie**ux**

5. Missing vowels – Section 5 and 6

a. **Lieux historiques** b. **Magasins** c. **Génial** d. **Plongée** e. **Connus** f. **Nul** g. **Je sortirai**

6. Choose the correct translation

a. Campagne: ***countryside*** b. Passer: ***to spend*** c. Lieux: ***places*** d. Louer: ***to rent*** e. Étoiles: ***stars***
f. Loger: ***to stay***

7. Complete with the correct option from the box

a. J'y passerai une **semaine** b. J'ai fait de la **plongée** c. Une auberge de **jeunesse**
d. Je voyagerai en **voiture** e. J'ai fait des visites **guidées** f. J'ai fait du **tourisme**

8. Break the flow

a. L'année dernière je suis allé au Portugal b. J'ai voyagé en avion puis j'ai loué une voiture
c. J'ai logé dans un hôtel au bord de la mer d. Le matin je suis allée à la plage. C'était relaxant
e. À midi j'ai mangé au restaurant de l'hôtel f. L'après-midi j'ai fait de la voile et de la plongée
g. J'ai aussi fait les magasins et du tourisme h. Le soir je suis sorti avec mon frère aîné

9. Split sentences

Je suis allée en **Allemagne** J'ai logé **dans un hôtel** J'y ai passé **une semaine** J'ai fait de **la natation**
Je suis allé au **Portugal** J'ai visité des **lieux historiques** J'ai fait du **tourisme**

10. Complete the table

Je louerai: *I will rent* J'ai loué: ***I rented*** **Je passerai**: *I will spend* J'ai passé: ***I spent***
J'ai logé: *I stayed* Je vais visiter: ***I am going to visit*** **J'ai fait**: *I did*

11. Find in the wordsearch the French for the words listed in the box below

Diving: **Plongée** *Evening*: **Soir** *Places*: **Lieux** *To rent*: **Louer** *Car*: **Voiture**
Countryside: **Campagne** *Great*: **Génial** *To spend*: **Passer**

12. Guided translation

a. **Le matin** b. **Je suis allé en boîte** c. **Lieux historiques** d. **J'ai fait du tourisme**
e. **J'ai passé une semaine** f. **Je visiterai** g. **Au bord de la mer** h. **Je ferai de la natation**
i. **Ce sera génial** j. **Ce sera relaxant** k. **Je passerai** l. **J'irai en Espagne**

13. Translate into French

a. **J'ai logé dans un hôtel trois étoiles au bord de la mer**
b. **J'ai voyagé en train et puis j'ai loué une voiture**
c. **Le matin, je suis allé(e) à la plage et ensuite j'ai fait du tourisme**
d. **J'ai visité beaucoup de lieux historiques et des musées**
e. **Je ferai de la plongée. Ce sera génial!**
f. **Je passerai deux semaines en Espagne**
g. **C'était très intéressant et relaxant**
h. **Le soir, je suis allé(e) en boîte avec mon frère aîné**

UNIT 10 - Test - Answers (/100)

1. Vocabulary recognition - French-to-English translation (/15)

a. ***I will travel***
b. ***Germany***
c. ***Afterwards/then***
d. ***I will spend***
e. ***A youth hostel***
f. ***I travelled***
g. ***By plane***
h. ***A car***
i. ***By the sea***
j. ***Days***
k. ***During***
l. ***This year***
m. ***In the summer***
n. ***In the countryside***
o. ***By car***

2. Syntax/Lexicogrammar – Split sentences (/5)

Tous les jours j'ai fait	**des visites guidées**
J'ai mangé	**au restaurant**
J'ai bronzé (sunbathed) à	**la plage**
Il y avait beaucoup	**de lieux historiques**
J'ai logé	**dans une auberge de jeunesse**

3. Grammar/Morphology/Vocabulary – Tangled translation (/20)

a. J'ai passé deux **semaines** en **Allemagne**
b. J'ai **visité** des **lieux** historiques
c. C'était très **intéressant**
d. **L'après-midi**, j'ai **bronzé** à la plage
e. C'était **vraiment** amusant et **relaxant**
f. Je **passerai** cinq jours à la **campagne**
g. **Pendant** les **vacances**, je suis allé en Grèce
h. À christmas, j'**irai** en France
i. Ce **sera** génial!
j. Le soir, **je suis sorti(e)** avec mes amis
k. Je **logerai** dans un hôtel quatre **étoiles**
l. Je **ferai** de la **plongée**

4. Translate into French (/ 60 – each full sentence – 6 points)

a. **L'année dernière, en été, je suis allé(e) en Espagne**
b. **J'ai voyagé en avion et puis j'ai loué une voiture**
c. **Nous avons logé dans un hôtel cinq étoiles au bord de la mer**
d. **Nous avons passé une semaine au Portugal. C'était amusant!**
e. **J'ai fait du tourisme et j'ai pris beaucoup de photos**
f. **Il y avait beaucoup de choses à faire et beaucoup de lieux/d'endroits à voir**
g. **L'année prochaine, j'irai en Allemagne. Je voyagerai en avion**
h. **Je logerai dans une auberge de jeunesse (2) à Berlin**
i. **Je visiterai des lieux historiques et des monuments connus. Ce sera génial!**
j. **Cet été, j'irai en Écosse et je voyagerai en voiture et puis je louerai un vélo**

Unit 11. Sport

KEY VOCABULARY Foundation

1. Les sports de ballon *(ball sports)*
J'ai joué... *I played...*
Je joue... *I play...*
Je jouerai... *I will play...*
-au basket: *basketball*
-au foot: *football*
-au ping-pong: *table tennis*

2. Les sports sans *(without)* ballon
J'ai fait... *I did...*
Je fais... *I do...*
Je ferai... *I will do...*
-de l'athlétisme: *athletics*
-de la boxe: *boxing*
-de la musculation: *bodybuilding*
-de la natation: *swimming*
-de la voile: *sailing*
-du footing: *jogging*
-du vélo: *cycling*

3. Si je pouvais... *If I could...*
Si je pouvais, je voudrais essayer...
If I could, I would like to try...
-l'escalade: *climbing*
-la plongée: *scuba diving*
-le parapente: *paragliding*
-le patin à glace: *ice skating*
-le ski: *skiing*

4. Les expressions de temps *(time)*
Une fois par semaine: *Once a week*
Tous les samedis: *Every Saturday*
Tous les week-ends: *Every weekend*
Après le collège: *After school*

5. Les endroits *(places)*
Je fais cela... *I do that...*
Je vais... *I go...*
-à la piscine: *at/to the swimming pool*
-au gymnase: *at/to the gym*
-au stade: *at/to the stadium*
-chez moi: *at home*

6. C'est comment? *How is it?*
Je trouve cela... *I find this...*
-compétitif: *competitive*
-divertissant: *entertaining*
-exaltant: *thrilling*
-passionnant: *exciting*
-risqué: *risky*

1. Match

Musculation	***Ice skating***
Natation	***Climbing***
Plongée	***Swimming***
Escalade	***Scuba diving***
Patin à glace	***Boxing***
Voile	***Bodybuilding***
Boxe	***Skiing***
Vélo	***Sailing***
Ski	***Cycling***

2. Translate into English

a. L'escalade

b. Le vélo

c. La voile

d. La plongée

e. Le parapente

f. Le patin à glace

g. La musculation

3. Gapped translation

a. Je voudrais essayer:
I would like to ___________

b. Une fois par semaine:
Once a ____________

c. Je ferai de la boxe:
I will do ____________

d. Si pouvais, je voudrais essayer:
__________, *I would like to try*

e. Je fais de la voile: *I do* _______

f. J'ai fait du vélo: *I went* _______

g. Je fais ça à la piscine:
I do this at the ________________

4. Missing vowels

a. L'_sc_l_de

b. La m_sc_l_t_ _ n

c. La pl_ng_ _

d. Le p_r_p_nt_

e. L_ p_sc_n_

f. Le g_mn_s_

g. Le st_d_

h. Le f_ _t_ng

5. Correct the wrong translations and tick the correct ones

a. L'escalade: *Skiing*
b. Fatigant: *Entertaining*
c. Divertissant: *Boring*
d. Samedi: *Saturday*
e. Le patin à glace: *Diving*
f. La piscine: *Gym*
g. Passionnant: *Exciting*
h. Si je pouvais: *If I did*
i. Essayer: *To buy*
j. La voile: *Boxing*
k. Le footing: *Jogging*
l. Je fais cela: *I try that*

6. Broken words

a. C'est un sport compé_ _ _ _ _
b. Une fois par sem_ _ _ _
c. Je fais ce_ _
d. C'est ex_ _ _ _ _ _
e. Je fais de la plon_ _ _
f. C'est fati_ _ _ _
g. Je fais de l'esca_ _ _ _
h. C'est passio_ _ _ _ _
i. Risq_ _
j. Le pa_ _ _ à glace

7. Break the flow

a. Jaimelanatationparcequejetrouvecelarelaxant

b. Jefaisdelamusculationchezmoitroisfoisparsemaine

c. Jenefaispasdesportparcequecestfatigant

d. Jejoueaurugbyetaufoottouslesjours

e. Jefaisduvélotouslesjoursaprèslecollège

f. Jevoudraisessayerleparapentecarcestrisqué

g. Jenaimepasfairedeléquitationcarcestennuyeux

h. Jetrouvelerugbypassionnantcarcestcompétitif

8. Complete with the missing words

a. Je voudrais ________ de l'escalade

b. Je ________ ce sport passionnant

c. Je ________ du vélo tous les jours

d. Je n'_______ pas ________ au rugby

e. Hier, j'ai ________ au foot

f. Je ne fais ______ de musculation parce que c'_______ fatigant

est	**fais**	**joué**	**jouer**
pas	**faire**	**trouve**	**aime**

9. Find in the wordsearch the French for the words listed in the box below

N	O	I	T	A	L	U	C	S	U	M
R	T	E	R	U	O	P	F	E	V	E
T	N	S	X	O	V	I	L	X	N	S
S	A	Q	U	A	É	C	H	U	H	S
U	N	S	J	H	L	P	Z	E	B	A
O	N	D	S	M	O	T	Q	Y	C	Y
L	O	I	D	T	G	A	T	U	A	E
R	I	S	Q	U	É	U	G	N	S	R
C	S	L	F	F	V	R	B	N	T	F
B	S	E	E	C	P	A	C	E	Z	P
O	A	R	E	D	A	L	A	C	S	E
T	P	L	O	N	G	É	E	J	D	V

Bodybulding: M
Cycling: V
Climbing: E
Exciting: P
Thrilling: E
Risky: R
Scuba diving: P
To try: E
Boring: E

10. Translate into French

a. Risky

b. Bodybuilding

c. I will do

d. If I could

e. I would like to try

f. Thrilling

g. It's competitive

h. Scuba diving

11. Gapped English-to-French translation

a. J'aime l'_________ parce que je _______ cela ___________ : *I like climbing because I find it exciting*

b. Je fais de la _________ chez ____ trois fois par ________ : *I do bodybuilding at home 3 times a week*

c. Je ne ______ pas de sport ______ que c'est __________ : *I don't do any sport because it's tiring*

d. Je _________ au tennis et au _______ tous les ___________ : *I play tennis and football every Sunday*

e. Je _________ du ________ tous les jours ________ le collège: *I go cycling every day after school*

f. Je voudrais ________ le parapente, car c'est ________ : *I'd like to try paragliding as it's risky*

g. Je n'aime pas la _______, car c'est ________ et ____ : *I don't like sailing as it's boring and rubbish*

h. Je trouve le rugby _____________, car c'est ____________ : *I find rugby exciting as it's competitive*

12. Translate into French

a. I do bodybuilding at home every day
b. I like football because it's thrilling
c. I play tennis three times a week
d. I don't like swimming because it's tiring
e. I don't like sailing because it's boring
f. I do jogging every Saturday because it's relaxing
g. I would like to try paragliding because it's risky

KEY VOCABULARY Higher

1. Le(s) sport(s) que je fais

Je fais... *I do...*
-de l'athlétisme: *athletics*
-de la musculation: *bodybuilding*
-de la natation: *swimming*
-de la voile: *sailing*
-du footing: *jogging*
-du vélo: *cycling*
Je joue... *I play...*
-au basket: *basketball*
-au foot: *football*

2. Pourquoi j'aime/je n'aime pas certains sports

Car c'est... *As it's...*
-amusant: *fun* / -compétitif: *competitive*
-divertissant: *entertaining*
-exaltant: *thrilling*
-fatigant: *tiring*
-risqué: *risky*

3. Quand je fais du sport *(when)*

Après le collège: *After school*
Tous les samedis: *Every Saturday*
Une fois par semaine: *Once a week*

4. Les lieux où je fais du sport *(places)*

Je fais cela… *I do this...*
-à la piscine: *at the swimming pool*
-au centre sportif: *at the sports centre*
-au gymnase: *at the gym*
-au stade: *at the stadium*

5. Le(s) sport(s) que j'ai fait hier

Hier, j'ai fait du vélo *Yesterday, I did cycling*
Le week-end dernier, j'ai joué au basket
Last weekend, I played basketball

6. Le(s) sport(s) que je ferai demain

Demain, je ferai de la natation
Tomorrow, I will do swimming
Le week-end prochain, je jouerai au foot
Next weekend, I will play football

7. Les sport que j'aimerais faire

Si je pouvais, je voudrais essayer...
If I could, I would like to try...
-la plongée: *scuba diving*
-le parapente: *paragliding*
-le patin à glace: *ice skating*

1. Match

Je fais du vélo	***I did sailing***
Je fais de la voile	***I played basketball***
Je jouerai au basket	***I do jogging***
J'ai fait du vélo	***I will do jogging***
Je ferai du footing	***I do sailing***
Je ferai de la voile	***I did cycling***
Je joue au basket	***I will do cycling***
Je ferai du vélo	***I will play basketball***
Je fais du footing	***I do cycling***
J'ai joué au basket	***I play basketball***
J'ai fait de la voile	***I will do sailing***
J'ai fait du footing	***I did jogging***

2. Broken words

a. Exalt_ _ _ : *Thrilling*
b. Ris_ _ _ : *Risky*
c. Foo_ _ _ _ : *Jogging*
d. St_ _ _ : *Stadium*
e. Pisc_ _ _ : *Pool*
f. Vé_ _ : *Bicycle*
g. Dem_ _ _ : *Tomorrow*
h. Vo_ _ _ : *Sailing*
i. Li_ _ _ : *Places*

3. Translate into English

a. Divertissant
b. Risqué
c. La voile
d. Une fois
e. Si je pouvais
f. Essayer
g. Je ferai
h. Fatigant
i. Parapente

4. Gapped translation

a. Hier, j'ai fait du vélo: *Yesterday, I did* __________
b. Je jouerai au basket: *I* _____________ *basketball*
c. Demain, je ferai de la voile: _________ *I will do sailing*
d. J'ai perdu le match: *I* __________ *the match*
e. Je ferai du sport: *I* ________ *do sport*
f. Je voudrais essayer: *I would like to* ______
g. J'irai à la piscine: *I* __________ *to the swimming pool*
h. J'ai fait de la plongée: *I* _________ *scuba diving*

5. Correct the wrong translation

a. La plongée: *Scuba diving*
b. Le vélo: *Sailing*
c. J'ai gagné: *I lost*
d. Le footing: *Cycling*
e. Je jouerai: *I played*
f. Stade: *Stadium*
g. Samedi: *Sunday*
h. Essayer: *To like*
i. Une fois: *One game*
j. Cela: *That*

6. Break the flow

a. Jefaiscelaàlapiscineunefoisparsemaine

b. Sijepouvaisjevoudraisessayerleparapente

c. Hierjaijouéautennisavecmonfrèreetjaigagné

d. Leweek-endprochainjeferaidelamusculation

e. Messportspréféréssontlescaladeetlevélo

f. Jevoudraisessayerlaplongéeetleparapente

g. Laplongéeestunsportrisquémaisfascinant

h. Dhabitudejementraînedeuxfoisparsemaine

7. Fill the gaps with the correct options

a. Le week-end __________, je ferai du _______

b. Hier, j'ai _______ au basket avec mes amis

c. Si je __________, je voudrais _________ le golf

d. Le parapente c'est _______ difficile!

e. Je m'__________ deux fois par _____________

f. D'___________, je ne fais pas de __________

pouvais	**entraîne**	**trop**	**semaine**	**essayer**
habitude	**joué**	**vélo**	**prochain**	**sport**

8. Find in the wordsearch the French words needed to complete the translations below

A	S	R	T	Y	I	P	Q	U	S	T	P	N
D	F	P	R	É	F	È	R	E	A	Z	C	V
E	H	E	R	Y	V	P	G	H	F	C	V	D
G	V	I	C	J	O	U	E	R	A	I	H	U
B	A	D	R	U	U	Y	P	V	I	C	G	C
J	Z	F	V	A	D	P	F	O	S	M	K	V
L	L	A	E	U	R	P	E	A	R	L	Q	A
N	I	I	T	Y	A	Y	R	T	I	A	H	J
S	F	T	U	O	I	T	A	Y	U	R		F
T	R	J	G	I	S	R	I	B	N	V	E	V
E	C	N	E	S	J	A	C	I	G	D	I	D
S	V	B	H	F	G	E	S	S	A	Y	E	R

I will do: Je __________

I will play: Je ______________

I did: J'ai _________

I would like to try: Je voudrais ___________

If I could: Si je ________

I would like: Je __________

I do: Je _______

I prefer: Je _________

9. Tangled translation

a. D'habitude, **I train** deux **times** par semaine

b. Le week-end **next**, je **will play** au badminton

c. Mon sport **favourite** est l'escalade parce que c'est **risky**

d. Si je **could**, je **would like** essayer la **scuba diving**

e. Je préfère les sport d'**team**, car c'est plus **competitive**

f. **Yesterday**, j'ai fait de la **sailing** et c'était **great**

g. Je ne joue **never** au golf parce que c'est **too** difficile

10. Translate into English

a. Génial

b. Essayer

c. Risqué

d. Parapente

e. Équipe

f. Musculation

g. Exaltant

11. Guided translation

a. *I never play*: J_ n_ j____ j______

b. *If I could*: S_ j_ p_________

c. *I will play*: J_ j___________

d. *It's more competitive*: C'e__ p__ c_________

e. *It's thrilling*: C'e___ e_____________

f. *I would like to try*: J_ v_______ e_________

g. *I train twice*: J_ m'__________ d____ f_____

h. *It looks fun*: C____ a l'a____ a_________

i. *I lost*: J'a_ p________

12. Translate into French

a. Yesterday, I played tennis and I lost

b. My favourite sport is athletics. It's fun!

c. I would like to try climbing as it's risky

d. I never play golf because it looks boring

e. I prefer team sports because it's more fun

f. Tomorrow, I will do bodybuilding with my sister

g. In the morning, I usually do jogging alone

h. Once a week, I play basketball at school

UNIT 11 - Test (/100)

1. Vocabulary recognition: French-to-English translation (/15)

a. Un sport d'équipe
b. D'habitude
c. Deux fois
d. Semaine
e. J'ai gagné
f. Hier
g. De temps en temps
h. La piscine
i. Divertissant
j. L'escalade
k. Exaltant
l. J'ai fait
m. La plongée
n. Une heure
o. Essayer

2. Syntax/Lexicogrammar – Split sentences (/5)

Je m'entraîne deux fois	de sport
Je préfère les sports	au ping-pong
Je ne fais pas	de la voile
J'ai joué	par semaine
J'ai fait	d'équipe

3. Grammar/Morphology/Vocabulary – Tangled translation (/20)

a. Tous les **Saturdays**, je fais de la **sailing**
b. Je **prefer** les sports individuels
c. Je **train** deux fois par semaine
d. J'ai **played** au ping-pong et **it was** amusant
e. Le week-end **last**, j'ai fait de la **boxing**
f. **Yesterday**, j'ai joué au tennis, mais **I lost**
g. Demain je **will play** au badminton avec mon **brother**
h. En général, Je m'entraîne **twice a week**
i. Je **go** à la **swimming pool** tous les dimanches
j. **Tomorrow**, je **will play** au foot avec mes amis
k. Mon sport **favourite** est l'**climbing**
l. C'est un sport un peu **risky**

4. Translate into French (/ 60 – each full sentence – 6 points)

a. I love ball sports like football and basketball
b. I can't stand team sports because they are boring
c. If I could, I would like to try climbing and swimming
d. I do it at the swimming pool four times a week
e. From time to time, I do bodybuilding. I do it at home
f. I would like to try paragliding because it's risky
g. I go to the gym and to the stadium once a week
h. I don't like jogging, because I find that it's too tiring
i. Tomorrow, I will play tennis with my older brother
j. I never play golf because it's too difficult and very expensive

Unit 11. Sport - Foundation - Answers

1. Match
Musculation – ***Bodybuilding*** Natation – ***Swimming*** Plongée – ***Scuba diving*** Escalade – ***Climbing***
Patin à glace – ***Ice skating*** Voile – ***Sailing*** Boxe – ***Boxing*** Vélo – ***Cycling*** Ski – ***Skiing***

2. Translate into English
a. ***Climbing*** b. ***Cycling*** c. ***Sailing*** d. ***Scuba diving*** e. ***Paragliding*** f. ***Ice skating*** g. ***Bodybuilding***

3. Gapped translation
a. *I would like to* ***try*** b. *Once a* ***week*** c. *I will do* ***boxing*** d. ***If I could****, I would like to try*
e. *I do* ***sailing*** f. *I went* ***cycling*** g. *I do this at the* ***swimming pool***

4. Missing vowels
a. **L'escalade** b. **La musculation** c. **La plongée** d. **Le parapente** e. **La piscine**
f. **Le gymnase** g. **Le stade** h. **Le footing**

5. Correct the wrong translations and tick the correct ones
a. L'escalade: ***Climbing*** b. Fatigant: ***Tiring*** c. Divertissant: ***Entertaining*** d. Samedi: *Saturday* e. Le patin à glace: ***Ice skating*** f. La piscine: ***Swimming pool*** g. Passionnant: *Exciting*
h. Si je pouvais: *If I* ***could*** i. Essayer: *To* ***try*** j. La voile: ***Sailing*** k. Le footing: *Jogging*
l. Je fais cela: *I* ***do this***

6. Broken words
a. C'est un sport compé**titif** b. Une fois par sem**aine** c. Je fais ce**la** d. C'est ex**altant**
e. Je fais de la plon**gée** f. C'est fati**gant** g. Je fais de l'esca**lade** h. C'est passio**nnant**
i. Risq**ué** j. Le pa**tin** à glace

7. Break the flow
a. J'aime la natation parce que je trouve cela relaxant
b. Je fais de la musculation chez moi trois fois par semaine c. Je ne fais pas de sport parce que c'est fatigant
d. Je joue au rugby et au foot tous les jours e. Je fais du vélo tous les jours après le collège
f. Je voudrais essayer le parapente car c'est risqué g. Je n'aime pas faire de l'équitation car c'est ennuyeux
h. Je trouve le rugby passionnant car c'est compétitif

8. Complete with the missing words
a. Je voudrais **faire** de l'escalade b. Je **trouve** ce sport passionnant c. Je **fais** du vélo tous les jours
d. Je n'**aime** pas **jouer** au rugby e. Hier, j'ai **joué** au foot
f. Je ne fais **pas** de musculation parce que c'**est** fatigant

9. Find in the wordsearch the French for the words listed in the box below
Bodybulding: **Musculation** *Cycling*: **Vélo** *Climbing*: **Escalade** *Exciting*: **Passionnant**
Thrilling: **Exaltant** *Risky*: **Risqué** *Scuba diving*: **Plongée** *To try*: **Essayer** *Boring*: **Ennuyeux**

10. Translate into French
a. **Risqué** b. **Musculation** c. **Je ferai** d. **Si je pouvais** e. **Je voudrais essayer**
f. **Exaltant** g. **C'est compétitif** h. **La plongée**

11. Gapped English-to-French translation
a. J'aime l'**escalade** parce que je **trouve** cela **passionnant**
b. Je fais de la **musculation** chez **moi** trois fois par **semaine**
c. Je ne **fais** pas de sport **parce** que c'est **fatigant**
d. Je **joue** au tennis et au **foot** tous les **dimanches**
e. Je **fais** du **vélo** tous les jours **après** le collège
f. Je voudrais **essayer** le parapente, car c'est **risqué**
g. Je n'aime pas la **voile**, car c'est **ennuyeux** et **nul**
h. Je trouve le rugby **passionnant**, car c'est **compétitif**

12. Translate into French
a. Je fais de la musculation chez moi tous les jours b. J'aime le foot parce que c'est exaltant
c. Je joue au tennis trois fois par semaine d. Je n'aime pas la natation parce que c'est fatigant
e. Je n'aime pas la voile parce que c'est ennuyeux
f. Je fais du footing tous les samedis parce que c'est relaxant
g. Je voudrais essayer le parapente, parce que c'est risqué

Unit 11. Sport - Higher - Answers

1. Match

Je fais du vélo – ***I do cycling*** Je fais de la voile – ***I do sailing*** Je jouerai au basket – ***I will play basketball***
J'ai fait du vélo – ***I did cycling*** Je ferai du footing – ***I will do jogging*** Je ferai de la voile – ***I will do sailing***
Je joue au basket – ***I play basketball*** Je ferai du vélo – ***I will do cycling*** Je fais du footing – ***I do jogging***
J'ai joué au basket – ***I played basketball*** J'ai fait de la voile – ***I did sailing***
J'ai fait du footing – ***I did jogging***

2. Broken words

a. Exalt**ant** b. Ris**qué** c. Foo**ting** d. Sta**de** e. Pisc**ine** f. Vé**lo** g. Dem**ain** h. Voi**le** i. Li**eux**

3. Translate into English

a. ***Entertaining*** b. ***Risky*** c. ***Sailing*** d. ***Once*** e. ***If I could*** f. ***To try*** g. ***I will do*** h. ***Tiring*** i. ***Paragliding***

4. Gapped translation

a. Hier j'ai fait du vélo: *Yesterday, I did* ***cycling*** b. Je jouerai au basket: *I* ***will play*** *basketball*
c. Demain, je ferai de la voile: ***Tomorrow,*** *I will do sailing* d. J'ai perdu le match: *I* ***lost*** *the match*
e. Je ferai du sport: *I* ***will*** *do sport* f. Je voudrais essayer: *I would like to* ***try***
g. J'irai à la piscine: *I* ***will go*** *to the swimming pool* h. J'ai fait de la plongée: *I* ***did*** *scuba diving*

5. Correct the wrong translation

a. La plongée: *Scuba diving* b. Le vélo: ***Cycling/Bicycle*** c. J'ai gagné: *I* ***won*** d. Le footing: ***Jogging***
e. Je jouerai: *I* ***will play*** f. Stade: *Stadium* g. Samedi: ***Saturday*** h. Essayer: *To* ***try*** i. Une fois: ***Once***
j. Cela: *that*

6. Break the flow

a. Je fais cela à la piscine une fois par semaine b. Si je pouvais je voudrais essayer le parapente
c. Hier j'ai joué au tennis avec mon frère et j'ai gagné d. Le week-end prochain je ferai de la musculation
e. Mes sports préférés sont l'escalade et le vélo f. Je voudrais essayer la plongée et le parapente
g. La plongée est un sport risqué mais fascinant h. D'habitude je m'entraîne deux fois par semaine

7. Fill the gaps with the correct options

a. Le week-end **prochain**, je ferai du **vélo** b. Hier, j'ai **joué** au basket avec mes amis
c. Si je **pouvais**, je voudrais **essayer** le golf d. Le parapente c'est **trop** difficile!
e. Je m'**entraîne** deux fois par **semaine** f. D'**habitude**, je ne fais pas de **sport**

8. Find in the wordsearch the French words needed to complete the translations below

I will do: Je **ferai** *I will play*: Je **jouerai** *I did*: J'ai **fait** *I would like to try*: Je voudrais **essayer**
If I could: Si je **pouvais** *I would like*: Je **voudrais** *I do*: Je **fais** *I prefer*: Je **préfère**

9. Tangled translation

a. D'habitude, **je m'entraîne** deux **fois** par semaine b. Le week-end **prochain**, je **jouerai** au badminton
c. Mon sport **préféré** est l'escalade parce que c'est **risqué** d. Si je **pouvais**, je **voudrais** essayer la **plongée**
e. Je préfère les sport d'**équipe**, car c'est plus **compétitif** f. **Hier**, j'ai fait de la **voile** et c'était **génial**
g. Je ne joue **jamais** au golf parce que c'est **trop** difficile

10. Translate into English

a. ***Great*** b. ***To try*** c. ***Risky*** d. ***Paragliding*** e. ***Team*** f. ***Bodybuilding*** g. ***Thrilling***

11. Guided translation

a. **Je ne joue jamais** b. **Si je pouvais** c. **Je jouerai** d. **C'est plus compétitif** e. **C'est exaltant**
f. **Je voudrais essayer** g. **Je m'entraîne deux fois** h. **Cela a l'air amusant** i. **J'ai perdu**

12. Translate into French

a. **Hier, j'ai joué au tennis et j'ai perdu** b. **Mon sport préféré est l'athlétisme. C'est amusant!**
c. **Je voudrais essayer l'escalade car c'est risqué** d. **Je ne joue jamais au golf car cela a l'air ennuyeux**
e. **Je préfère les sports d'équipe parce que c'est plus amusant**
f. **Demain, je ferai de la musculation avec ma sœur** g. **Le matin, d'habitude je fais du footing seul(e)**
h. **Une fois par semaine, je joue au basket à l'école/au collège**

UNIT 11 - Test - Answers (/100)

1. Vocabulary recognition: French-to-English translation (/15)

a. ***A team sport***
b. ***Usually***
c. ***Twice/Two times***
d. ***Week***
e. ***I won***
f. ***Yesterday***
g. ***From time to time***
h. ***The swimming pool***
i. ***Entertaining***
j. ***Climbing***
k. ***Thrilling***
l. ***I did***
m. ***Scuba diving***
n. ***An/One hour***
o. ***To try***

2. Syntax/Lexicogrammar – Split sentences (/5)

Je m'entraîne deux fois	**par semaine**
Je préfère les sports	**d'équipe**
Je ne fais pas	**de sport**
J'ai joué	**au ping-pong**
J'ai fait	**de la voile**

3. Grammar/Morphology/Vocabulary – Tangled translation (/20)

a. Tous les **samedis**, je fais de la **voile**
b. Je **préfère** les sports individuels
c. Je **m'entraîne** deux fois par semaine
d. J'ai **joué** au ping-pong et **c'était** amusant
e. Le week-end **dernier**, j'ai fait de la **boxe**
f. **Hier**, j'ai joué au tennis, mais **j'ai perdu**
g. Demain je **jouerai** au badminton avec mon **frère**
h. En général, Je m'entraîne **deux fois par semaine**
i. Je **vais** à la **piscine** tous les dimanches
j. **Demain**, je **jouerai** au foot avec mes amis
k. Mon sport **préféré** est l'**escalade**
l. C'est un sport un peu **risqué**

4. Translate into French (/ 60 – each full sentence – 6 points)

a. **J'adore les sports de ballon comme le foot et le basket**
b. **Je ne supporte pas (2) les sports d'équipe parce qu' ils sont ennuyeux**
c. **Si je pouvais, je voudrais essayer l'escalade et la natation**
d. **Je fais cela à la piscine quatre fois par semaine**
e. **De temps en temps (2), je fais de la musculation. Je fais cela chez moi**
f. **Je voudrais essayer le parapente parce que c'est risqué**
g. **Je vais au gymnase et au stade une fois par semaine**
h. **Je n'aime pas le footing, parce que je trouve que c'est trop fatigant**
i. **Demain, je jouerai au tennis avec mon frère aîné**
j. **Je ne joue jamais (2) au golf parce que c'est trop difficile et très cher**

Unit 12. Customs and festivals

KEY VOCABULARY Foundation

1. Les fêtes *(festivals)*
Chaque année, nous fêtons...
Each year, we celebrate...
- la fête des mères/pères *Mother's/Father's Day*
-la fête des rois: *the Epiphany*
-la Saint-Valentin: *Valentine's Day*
-l'Aïd al-Fitr: *Eid al-Fitr*
-le jour de l'an: *New Year's Day*
-Noël: *Christmas*
-Pâques *Easter*

2. Les religions et les lieux de culte
Les chrétiens: *The Christians*
Les juifs: *The Jews*
Les musulmans: *The Muslims*
La mosquée: *The mosque*
La synagogue: *The synagogue*
L'église: *The church*
Les hindous: *The Hindus*
Prier Dieu: *To pray to God*

3. Les expressions de temps
Pendant les fêtes religieuses
During religious festivals
Chaque année : *Each year*

4. Les expressions essentielles
Les gens… *People…*
-sont en congé : *are on holidays*
-offrent des cadeaux : *offer gifts*
-se réunissent : *get together*
-se rencontrent : *meet*
C'est ma fête préférée parce que…
It's my favourite festival because…
-je reçois des cadeaux : *I receive gifts*
-je suis en vacances : *I am on holidays*
-je vois ma famille/mes amis/mes cousins
I see my family/my friends/my cousins
Des jours fériés: *Public holidays*
Un repas de fête: *A festive meal*

5. Évènements *(events)*
Dans la plupart des villes, il y a...
In most cities, there are...
-des concerts: *concerts*
-des défilés: *processions*
-des feux d'artifice: *fireworks*

1. Match

Pâques	***New Year's Day***
La fête des rois	***During festivals***
Le jour de l'an	***The Epiphany***
Noël	***Christians***
Les chrétiens	***Easter***
Pendant les fêtes	***People***
Les juifs	***Christmas***
Prier Dieu	***The Jews***
Les gens	***To pray to God***
Les cadeaux	***Gifts***

2. Broken words

a. L'égli_ _ : *Church*
b. Di_ _ : *God*
c. Cad_ _ _ _ : *Gifts*
d. La mosq_ _ _ : *Mosque*
e. Le jo_ _ de l'an: *New Year's day*
f. Pâq_ _ _ : *Easter*
g. Pr_ _ _ : *To pray*
h. No_ _ : *Christmas*

3. Translate into English

a. La fête des rois
b. Les chrétiens
c. Les gens
d. Le jour de l'an
e. Cadeaux
f. Je reçois
g. L'église
h. La Saint-Valentin
i. Noël

4. Gapped translation

a. Les gens offrent des cadeaux: *People offer* ________
b. C'est ma fête préférée: *It's my favourite* __________
c. Je vais à l'église: *I go to* __________
d. Je vois ma famille: *I* _______ *my family*
e. Nous fêtons Noël: *We* __________ *Christmas*
f. Je suis en vacances: *I am on* __________
g. Je reçois des cadeaux: *I* _________ *gifts*
h. Un repas de fête: *A festive* __________

5. Correct the wrong translation

a. Les gens: *Gifts*
b. Les défilés: *Processions*
c. Je vois: *I drink*
d. Un repas: *A meal*
e. Chaque: *Easter*
f. Cadeaux: *Fireworks*
g. Fête: *Festival*
h. Église: *Church*
i. Pâques: *Easter*
j. Feux d'artifice: *Concerts*

6. Break the flow

a. Pendantlesfêtesimportanteslesgensserencontrent

b. ÀNoëljereçoisdescadeaux

c. Jadorelesrepasdefête

d. Lejourdelanjaimeregarderlesfeuxdartifice

e. Pâquescestmafêtepréférée

f. Jevaisàlamosquéeavecmonpèreetmesfrères

g. Chaqueannéeenjanviernousfêtonslafêtedesrois

h. Dansmavilleilyadesdéfilésetdesconcerts

7. Fill the gaps with the correct options

a. Le jour de l'____ il y a des feux d'artifice

b. Ma ________ préférée, c'est l'Aïd al-Fitr

c. À Pâques, je mange des _____ au chocolat

d. À Noël, je reçois beaucoup de ________

e. Chaque année nous _______ l'Aïd al-Fitr

f. À Noël, les ________ se rencontrent

an	**œufs**	**gens**
fêtons	**cadeaux**	**fête**

8. Find in the wordsearch the French for the words listed in the box below

Q	U	E	R	S	D	E	A	R	P	L	V	F
A	U	C	H	R	É	T	I	E	N	S	F	Ê
D	I	E	A	U	F	N	M	A	O	S	I	T
Z	Y	Z	Q	T	I	D	G	V	U	P	J	E
F	A	S	C	P	L	R	F	G	S	M	B	D
H	O	B	S	I	É	C	F	H	F	P	T	E
M	R	E	P	A	S	D	E	F	Ê	T	E	S
D	L	J	U	T	F	S	U	G	T	A	Z	R
F	S	O	P	U	I	V	P	P	O	N	Q	O
H	T	M	T	A	U	T	Y	E	N	M	A	I
Z	R	B	N	D	J	U	N	Z	P	D	P	S
A	R	T	I	F	I	C	E	C	V	H	B	D

The Christians: Les ____________

The Jews: Les ____________

Epiphany: La _______ ___ _____

Processions: Les d__________

Festive meals: Les _______ ___ _______

Mosque: ___________

Fireworks: Les feux d'__________

We celebrate: _____ ___________

9. Tangled translation

a. Il y a des **processions** et **some** concerts

b. Nous **celebrate** Noël et **Easter**

c. Ma fête **favourite,** c'est la **Valentine's Day**

d. Ce que **I like** le plus, c'est les **fireworks**

e. Le **New Year's Day**, nous mangeons **a lot**. J'adore les **festive meals**!

f. A Noël, je **receive** beaucoup de **gifts**

g. Dans la **most** des **towns**, il y a des concerts

h. À **Christmas**, les familles se **get together**

10. Translanagrams – Work out the hidden words and translate them into English

a. eLs osRi: Les Rois - *The kings*

b. eLs enschréti:

c. nU asrep de tefê:

d. esqPâu:

e. eLs jfsui:

f. aL quéesom:

g. seL caauxde de ëlNo:

h. Nuso nsfêto:

11. Guided translation

a. P_ _ _ _ _ : *Easter*

b. L_j_ _ _ d_ l'a_ : *New Year's Day*

c. N_ _ _ : *Christmas*

d. L_ _ j_ _ _ _ : *The Jews*

e. L_ _ r_ _ _ _ d_ f_ _ _ : *Festive meals*

f. J_ r_ _ _ _ _ d_ _ c_ _ _ _ _ _ : *I receive gifts*

g. I_ y a d_ _ d_ _ _ _ _ _ : *There are processions*

12. Translate into French

a. Every year, we celebrate Eid al-Fitr

b. I love Christmas because I receive gifts

c. Valentine's Day is my favourite festival

d. I love watching fireworks during festivals

e. On New Year's Day people get together and eat a festive meal together

f. In most towns there are processions

g. I go to church with my family at Easter

KEY VOCABULARY Higher

1. Les fêtes

Chaque année... *Each year...*
Le 25 décembre...
On the 25th December...
Chez moi... *At home...*
Nous fêtons... *We celebrate*
-l'Aïd al-Fitr: *Eid al-Fitr*
-la fête des mères/pères *Mother's/Father's Day*
-la fête des rois: *the Epiphany*
-la Saint-Valentin: *Valentine's Day*
-le jour de l'an: *New Year's Day*
-Noël: *Christmas* / -Pâques: *Easter*
-des jours feriés: *public holidays*

2. Où l'on va pendant les fêtes religieuses

Pendant les fêtes religieuses...
During religious festivals...
-les chrétiens: *the Christians*
-les hindous: *the Hindus*
-les juifs: *the Jews*
-les musulmans: *the Muslims*
...vont... *...go...*
-à l'église: *to the church*
-à la mosquée: *to the mosque*
-à la synagogue: *to the synagogue*
-au temple: *to the temple*

3. Ce qu'on fait pendant les fêtes

Les gens offrent des cadeaux à leurs…
People offer gifts to their...
-enfants: *children* / -proches: *relatives*
Les amis/Les familles…
Friends/families...
-s'appellent: *call each other*
-se rencontrent: *meet*
-se réunissent: *get together*
...pour… *...in order to...*
…dîner/fêter/manger ensemble
...dine/celebrate/eat together
Dans la plupart des villes il y a…
In most towns there are...
-des défilés: *processions*
-des feux d'artifice: *fireworks*

4. Ma fête préférée

Ma fête préférée, c'est... parce que…
My favourite festival is... because...
-je reçois des cadeaux: *I receive gifts*
-je ne vais pas à l'école *I don't go to school*
-je suis en vacances: *I am on holidays*
-je vois mes proches/mes amis/cousins
I see my relatives/friends/cousins

1. Match

Chez moi	***Gifts***
Pâques	***New Year's Day***
La fête	***People***
Le jour de l'an	***Christmas***
Noël	***Church***
Les musulmans	***The Christians***
Les gens	***Each***
L'église	***At home***
Les chrétiens	***The Muslims***
Chaque	***Festival/Party***
Les enfants	***Easter***
Les cadeaux	***Children***
Les proches	***Relatives***

2. Gapped translation

a. Nous fêtons le jour de l'an: *We celebrate* ____________

b. Ils vont à l'église: *They go to the* ___________

c. Les gens offrent: ________ *give/offer*

d. Pendant les fêtes: *During the* ____________

e. Les amis se recontrent: *Friends* ____________

f. Les gens se réunissent: *People* __________

g. Fêter et dîner ensemble: *To celebrate and dine* _________

h. Il y a des défilés: *There are* _____________

3. Translate into English

a. Les amis se rencontrent pour dîner ensemble

b. Les gens se réunissent avec leurs proches

c. Les musulmans vont à la mosquée

d. Dans la plupart des villes, il y a des défilés

e. Pendant les fêtes, je vois mes proches

f. Je ne vais pas à l'école

g. Les gens offrent des cadeaux

4. Broken words

a. N_ _l

b. L'égli_ _

c. Des défi_ _s

d. Mes proch_ _

e. Les fe_ _ d'artifice

f. Les am_ _

g. Les cade_ _ _

h. Les gen_

5. Missing vowels

a. M_sq_ _ _ : *Mosque*
b. D_ f_l_s: *Processions*
c. _c_l_ : *School*
d. Pr_ch_s: *Relatives*
e. _gl_s_ : *Church*
f. _nf_nts: *Children*
g. P_qu_s: *Easter*

6. Choose the correct translation

a. **Noël**: Easter / Passover / Christmas

b. **Passer**: to spend / to rent / to buy

c. **Pâques**: Easter / Places / Passover

d. **Fêter**: to spend / to stay / to celebrate

e. **Église**: mosque / church / gift

f. **Cadeaux**: gifts / children / people

7. Complete with the correct option from the box

a. Je passe Pâques en __________

b. __ 25 décembre, c'est Noël

c. Je vais à la _________

d. Les gens offrent des _________

e. Ma ____ préférée c'est le jour de l'an

f. Les gens se réunissent et dînent ____________

ensemble
famille
fête
cadeaux
le
mosquée

8. Break the flow

a. Chaqueannéelevingt-cinqdécembrenousfêtonsNoël

b. MafêtepréféréecestlAïdal-Fitr

c. Pendantlesfêtesreligieuseslesgensseréunissent

d. Leschrétiensvontàléglisetlesmusulmansàlamosquée

e. Lesparentsdonnentdescadeauxàleursenfants

f. Danslaplupartdesvillesilyadesconcertsetdesdéfilés

g. Jadorelesfeuxdartifice

h. Lafêtedesroiscestlesixjanvier

9. Definition game

a. Une fête musulmane: L'A

b. Une fête chrétienne: P

c. On les offre aux enfant à Noël: C

d. La fête de l'amour: La S

e. Le verbe des fêtes: F

f. Un lieu de culte juif: S

g. Un lieu de culte chrétien: É

10. Complete the table

English	Français
	Jours fériés
New Year's Day	
	Les fêtes religieuses
People give	
People meet	
	Je vois
	Feux d'artifice
In most cities	
	Dîner ensemble

11. Translate into French

a. *Children*: E

b. *Relatives*: P

c. *Together*: E

d. *Fireworks*: F

e. *Processions*: D

f. *Christians*: C

g. *At home*: C

h. *Public Holidays*: J

i. *Most*: La p

j. *To celebrate*: F

k. *To dine*: D

l. *To spend*: P

m. *Christmas*: N

n. *Muslims*: M

o. *Parents*: P

p. *Easter*: P

q. *Mosque*: M

r. *People*: G

12. Translate into French

a. Muslims go to the mosque and Jews go to the synagogue

b. During the festivals I see my relatives

c. In most towns there are fireworks, processions and concerts

d. On the 25th December, we celebrate Christmas

e. People meet and eat a festive meal together

f. My favourite festival is Easter because I eat chocolate eggs

g. I receive gifts from my parents and my grandparents

h. I love Valentine's Day because I am romantic

i. I love Christmas because I have long holidays

UNIT 12 - Test (/100)

1. Vocabulary recognition: French-to-English translation (/15)

a. Les juifs	f. Leur	k. Je reçois
b. Les chrétiens	g. Les fêtes	l. Des défilés
c. Prier	h. Cadeaux	m. Feux d'artifice
d. Dieu	i. Bon	n. Je vois
e. Proches	j. Un repas	o. Les gens

2. Syntax/Lexicogrammar – Split sentences (/5)

Je suis	jour de l'an
Les gens se réunissent pour	en vacances
J'aime regarder	partager un bon moment
Nous fêtons le	à leur proches
Les gens offrent des cadeaux	les feux d'artifice

3. Grammar/Morphology/Vocabulary – Tangled translation (/20)

a. Nous **celebrate** la **festival** des mères

b. **During** les fêtes **religious**

c. Les **people** offrent des **gifts** à leurs proches

d. Nous **go** à l'**church**

e. **I don't go** à l'**school**

f. **Usually**, ce sont des **public holidays**

g. Les gens **eat** un repas festif avec leurs **relatives**

h. Les gens **get together**

i. **In most** villes, il y a des processions

j. Ma fête **favourite**, c'est **Easter**

k. Il y a des **fireworks**, c'est génial!

l. À Noël, d'habitude, **I see** tous mes oncles et tantes

4. Translate into French (/ 60 – each full sentence – 6 points)

a. At Christmas, parents offer gifts to their children

b. Families get together to dine and celebrate the occasion together

c. On 6th January, the Christians celebrate Epiphany

d. During most religious festivals we don't go to school

e. My favourite festival is Eid al-Fitr because I see my cousins

f. In most cities there are processions, concerts and fireworks

g. During Passover (Paque/Pessah), the Jews go to the synagogue to pray to their God

h. I love Valentine's Day because my boyfriend gives me a gift

i. We get together at my house to share a good time

j. In my family, we celebrate Christmas, New Year's Day and Easter

Unit 12. Customs and festivals - Foundation - Answers

1. Match

Pâques – ***Easter*** La fête des rois – ***The Epiphany*** Le jour de l'an – ***New Year's Day*** Noël – ***Christmas***
Les chrétiens – ***Christians*** Pendant les fêtes – ***During festivals*** Les juifs – ***The Jews***
Prier Dieu – ***To pray to God*** Les gens – ***People*** Les cadeaux – ***Gifts***

2. Broken words

a. L'ég**lise** b. Di**eu** c. Cad**eaux** d. La mosq**uée** e. Le jo**ur** de l'an f. Paq**ues** g. Pri**er** h. No**ël**

3. Translate into English

a. ***The Epiphany*** b. ***The Christians*** c. ***People*** d. ***New Year's Day*** e. ***Gifts***
f. ***I receive*** g. ***The church*** h. ***Valentine's Day*** i. ***Christmas***

4. Gapped translation

a. *People offer **gifts*** b. *It's my favourite **festival*** c. *I go to **church*** d. *I **see** my family*
e. *We **celebrate** Christmas* f. *I am on **holidays*** g. *I **receive** gifts* h. *A festive **meal***

5. Correct the wrong translation

a. Les gens: ***People*** b. Les défilés: *Processions* c. Je vois: *I **see*** d. Un repas: *A meal* e. Chaque: ***Each*** f. Cadeaux: ***Gifts*** g. Fête: *Festival* h. Église: *Church* i. Pâques: *Easter* j. Feux d'artifice: ***Fireworks***

6. Break the flow

a. Pendant les fêtes importantes les gens se rencontrent b. À Noël je reçois des cadeaux
c. J'adore les repas de fête d. Le jour de l'an j'aime regarder les feux d'artifice
e. Pâques c'est ma fête préférée f. Je vais à la mosquée avec mon père et mes frères
g. Chaque année en janvier nous fêtons la fête des rois h. Dans ma ville il y a des défilés et des concerts

7. Fill the gaps with the correct options

a. Le jour de l'**an** il y a des feux d'artifice b. Ma **fête** préférée, c'est l'Aïd al-Fitr
c. À Pâques je mange des **œufs** au chocolat d. À Noël, je reçois beaucoup de **cadeaux**
e. Chaque année nous **fêtons** l'Aïd al-Fitr f. À Noël, les **gens** se rencontrent

8. Find in the wordsearch the French for the words listed in the box below

The Christians: Les **chrétiens** *The Jews*: Les **juifs** *Epiphany*: La **fête des rois** *Processions*: Les **défilés**
Festive meals: Les **repas de fête** *Mosque*: **Mosquée** *Fireworks*: Les feux d'**artifice**
We celebrate: **Nous fêtons**

9. Tangled translation

a. Il y a des **défilés** et **des** concerts b. Nous **fêtons** Noël et **Pâques**
c. Ma fête **préférée,** c'est la **Saint-Valentin** d. Ce que **j'aime** le plus, c'est les **feux d'artifice**
e. Le **jour de l'an**, nous mangeons **beaucoup**. J'adore les **repas de fête**!
f. A Noël, je **reçois** beaucoup de **cadeaux** g. Dans la **plupart** des **villes**, il y a des concerts
h. À **Noël**, les familles se **réunissent**

10. Translanagrams – Work out the hidden words and translate them into English

a. eLs osRi: Les Rois - *The kings* b. **Les chrétiens**: ***The Christians*** c. **Un repas de fête**: ***A festive meal***
d. **Pâques**: ***Easter*** e. **Les juifs**: ***The Jews*** f. **La mosquée**: ***The mosque***
g. **Les cadeaux de Noël**: ***Christmas gifts*** h. **Nous fêtons**: ***We celebrate***

11. Guided translation

a. **Pâques** b. **Le jour de l'an** c. **Noël** d. **Les juifs** e. **Les repas de fête**
f. **Je reçois des cadeaux** g. **Il y a des défilés**

12. Translate into French

a. **Chaque année, nous fêtons l'Aïd al-Fitr**
b. **J'adore Noël parce que je reçois des cadeaux**
c. **La Saint-Valentin est ma fête préférée**
d. **J'adore regarder les feux d'artifice pendant les fêtes**
e. **Le premier de l'an, les gens se réunissent et mange un repas de fête ensemble**
f. **Dans la plupart des villes, il y a des défilés**
g. **Je vais à l'église avec ma famille à Pâques**

Unit 12. Customs and festivals - Higher - Answers

1. Match

Chez moi – ***At home*** Pâques – ***Easter*** La fête – ***Festival/Party*** Le jour de l'an – ***New Year's Day*** Noël – ***Christmas*** Les musulmans – ***The Muslims*** Les gens – ***People*** L'église – ***Church*** Les chrétiens – ***The Christians*** Chaque – ***Each*** Les enfants – ***Children*** Les cadeaux – ***Gifts*** Les proches – ***Relatives***

2. Gapped translation

a. *We celebrate* ***New Year's Day*** b. *They go to the* ***church*** c. ***People*** *give/offer*
d. *During the* ***festivals/parties*** e. *Friends* ***meet*** f. *People* ***get together***
g. *To celebrate and dine* ***together*** h. *There are* ***processions***

3. Translate into English

a. ***Friends meet to dine together*** b. ***People get together with their relatives***
c. ***The Muslims go to the mosque*** d. ***In most cities, there are processions***
e. ***During festivals, I see my relatives*** f. ***I don't go to school*** g. ***People offer gifts***

4. Broken words

a. No**ël** b. L'égli**se** c. Des défil**és** d. Mes proch**es** e. Les fe**ux** d'artifice f. Les am**is**
g. Les cade**aux** h. Les ge**ns**

5. Missing vowels

a. **Mosquée** b. **Défilés** c. **École** d. **Proches** e. **Église** f. **Enfants** g. **Pâques**

6. Choose the correct translation

a. Noël: ***Christmas*** b. Passer: ***to spend*** c. Pâques: ***Easter*** d. Fêter: ***to celebrate***
e. Église: ***church*** f. Cadeaux: ***gifts***

7. Complete with the correct option from the box

a. Je passe Pâques en **famille** b. **Le** 25 décembre, c'est Noël c. Je vais à la **mosquée**
d. Les gens offrent des **cadeaux** e. Ma **fête** préférée c'est le jour de l'an
f. Les gens se réunissent et dînent **ensemble**

8. Break the flow

a. Chaque année le vingt-cinq décembre nous fêtons Noël b. Ma fête préférée c'est l'Aïd al-Fitr
c. Pendant les fêtes religieuses les gens se réunissent
d. Les chrétiens vont à l'église et les musulmans à la mosquée
e. Les parents donnent des cadeaux à leurs enfants
f. Dans la plupart des villes il y a des concerts et des défilés g. J'adore les feux d'artifice
h. La fête des rois c'est le six janvier

9. Definition game

a. L'**Aïd al-Fitr** b. **Pâques** c. **Cadeaux** d. **La Saint-Valentin** e. **Fêter** f. **Synagogue** g. **Église**

10. Complete the table

Public holidays: Jours fériés *New Year's Day*: **Le jour de l'an** ***Religious festivals***: Les fêtes religieuses
People give: **Les gens donnent** *People meet*: **Les gens se rencontrent** ***I see***: Je vois
Fireworks: Feux d'artifice *In most cities*: **Dans la plupart des villes** ***To dine together***: Dîner ensemble

11. Translate into French

a. **Enfants** b. **Proches** c. **Ensemble** d. **Feux d'artifice** e. **Défilés** f. **Chrétiens** g. **Chez moi**
h. **Jours fériés** i. **La plupart** j. **Fêter** k. **Dîner** l. **Passer** m. **Noël** n. **Musulmans** o. **Parents**
p. **Pâques** q. **Mosquée** r. **Gens**

12. Translate into French

a. **Les musulmans vont à la mosquée et les juifs vont à la synagogue**
b. **Pendant les fêtes je vois mes proches**
c. **Dans la plupart des villes il y a des feux d'artifice, des défilés et des concerts**
d. **Le 25 décembre, nous fêtons Noël**
e. **Les gens se rencontrent et mangent un repas de fête ensemble**
f. **Ma fête préférée est Pâques parce que je mange des œufs en chocolat**
g. **Je reçois des cadeaux de mes parents et de mes grands-parents**
h. **J'adore la Saint-Valentin parce que je suis romantique**
i. **J'adore Noël parce que j'ai de longues vacances**

UNIT 12 - Test - Answers (/100)

1. Vocabulary recognition: French-to-English translation (/15)

a. ***The Jews***

b. ***The Christians***

c. ***To pray***

d. ***God***

e. ***Relatives***

f. ***Their***

g. ***Festivals***

h. ***Gifts/Presents***

i. ***Good***

j. ***A meal***

k. ***I receive***

l. ***Processions***

m. ***Fireworks***

n. ***I see***

o. ***People***

2. Syntax/Lexicogrammar – Split sentences (/5)

Je suis	**en vacances**
Les gens se réunissent pour	**partager un bon moment**
J'aime regarder	**les feux d'artifice**
Nous fêtons le	**jour de l'an**
Les gens offrent des cadeaux	**à leur proches**

3. Grammar/Morphology/Vocabulary – Tangled translation (/20)

a. Nous **fêtons** la **fête** des mères

b. **Pendant** les fêtes **religieuses**

c. Les **gens** offrent des **cadeaux** à leurs proches

d. Nous **allons** à l'**église**

e. **Je ne vais pas** à l'**école**

f. **D'habitude**, ce sont des **jours fériés**

g. Les gens **mangent** un repas festif avec leurs **proches**

h. Les gens **se réunissent**

i. **Dans la plupart des** villes, il y a des processions

j. Ma fête **préférée/favorite**, c'est **Pâques**

k. Il y a des **feux d'artifice**, c'est génial!

l. À Noël, d'habitude, **je vois** tous mes oncles et tantes

4. Translate into French (/ 60 – each full sentence – 6 points)

a. **À Noël, les parents offrent/donnent des cadeaux à leurs enfants**

b. **Les familles se réunissent pour dîner et fêter l'occasion ensemble**

c. **Le six janvier (2), les chrétiens fêtent la fête des rois (2)**

d. **Pendant la plupart des fêtes religieuses, nous n'allons pas (2) à l'école**

e. **Ma fête préférée/favorite est l'Aïd al-Fitr parce que je vois mes cousins**

f. **Dans la plupart des villes, (2) il y a des défilés, des concerts et des feux d'artifice**

g. **Pendant Paque/Pessah, les juifs vont à la synagogue pour prier leur Dieu**

h. **J'adore la Saint-Valentin parce que mon petit ami me donne un cadeau**

i. **Nous nous réunissons (2) chez moi/dans ma maison pour partager un bon moment (2)**

j. **Dans ma famille, nous fêtons Noël, le jour de l'an et Pâques**

Made in United States
North Haven, CT
11 June 2023

37616911R00057